LOVE BLOOMS
AMONG THE RUINS

LOVE BLOOMS
AMONG THE RUINS

Daniel Jami

The Inayati-Maimuni Order
Boulder, Colorado
2023

*"The old shall be renewed,
and the new shall be made holy."*
— Rabbi Avraham Yitzhak Kook

This book has been produced for the Inayati-Maimuni Order in cooperation with Albion-Andalus Books.

Albion-Andalus Inc.
P. O. Box 19852
Boulder, CO 80308
www.albionandalus.com

Design and composition by Albion-Andalus Books

Cover designed in collaboration with Meagan Rabi'a Santangelo

Cover Image of *'Layla and Majnun in the wilderness with animals, from a Khamsa (Quintet) of Amir Khusrau Dihlavi,'* Gum tempera, ink, and gold on paper, attributed to Sanwalah (CC0 license issued by the Cleveland Musuem of Art).

Illustrations by Edward Sullivan, from Edward Fitzgerald's translation of Omar Khayyam's *Rubaiyat.*

ISBN-13: 978-1-953220-28-8 (Paperback)

Manufactured in the United States of America

For You

Contents

"If you are everything,
then who are all these people?
And if I am nothing,
what's all this noise about?
You are Totality; everything is You. Agreed.
Then that which is 'other-than-You,' what is it?
Oh, indeed I know: nothing exists but You.
But tell me: why the confusion?"

— Fakhruddin 'Iraqi, *Divine Flashes*

INTRODUCTION

Friend—

The collection of poems you find yourself holding forms a sort of spiritual journal, written over a roughly four-year period, in a voice not entirely my own. During this time, one of the hardest of my life, my deepest stirrings felt most easily expressed under the guise of 'Jami,' a Sufi love-poet, fool, and would-be-teacher. Though a character of sorts, 'Jami' is also my Sufi initiatory name and a vessel for authentic personal expression. Though nonsensical, there is only one way to say it truthfully: Jami both is and is not 'me.'

As these poems participate in the Sufi tradition of poetry, with its rich diversity of symbols, myth, and culture, I want to provide some context for the Sufi orientation from which this work speaks. By 'Sufi,' I mean a practitioner of Sufism, the definition of which exists in many iterations, as creating such definitions has itself long been a Sufi practice. For example, Sufism is "a 1,400 year-old mystical tradition with origins in the Middle East, which uses the transformative power of love and remembrance to create change in the individual's consciousness;" it is "a school of experience, not dogma," "the religion of love," and "the process of awakening and developing latent human powers under divine grace and guidance."[1]

My connection to this tradition lies in my relationship to the Sufi master Pir Netanel Mu'in ad-Din Miles-Yépez, and the community he leads, the Inayati-Maimuni Order. For more than a millennium, Sufism has organized itself into orders or lineages *(tariqat)* that often acquire the name of their founder. Hence, the first half of our order's name, 'Inayati,' indicates a universalist Sufi order in the lineage of Sufi master Hazrat Inayat Khan (1882-1927)—a genius musician and teacher of the Chishti Sufi order, who in 1910 left India at his teacher's direction, and spent the rest of his life in Europe and America teaching Sufism.

For the most part, Sufism has been a mystical tradition existing alongside and fully integrated with Islam and Islamic culture. Indeed, many would rightfully define Sufism as a mystical path within Islam. But in the West, Hazrat Inayat Khan began teaching a Sufism that did not require conversion, and in the process, produced an extensive collection of universalist Sufi teachings and a network of universalist Sufism, open to people of any (or even no) religious or spiritual affiliation.

Hence, despite this work riffing on themes and motifs from great Sufi poets, the overwhelming majority of whom have been Muslims speaking from an Islamic Sufi perspective, it emerges from a universalist lens and Sufi community. Despite being informed by Islamic teachings, these poems are like myself—not bound to one religion in particular, and open to wisdom from the many divinely inspired messengers across place and time, between whom, based on the Qur'an's example, we do not make distinctions of value.[2]

The 'Inayati,' in the Inayati-Maimuni Order to which I belong, indicates this universalist Sufism, and my own 'Sufi location,' if you will; but so does 'Maimuni,' the second half of the name, indicating a specific Inayati branch. Not only are we the universalist rainbow-headed step-children of Islamic Sufism, even among universalist Sufis our hyphen makes us an oddity. For the 'Maimuni' side comes from Pir Netanel's teacher, and co-founder of the order, Rabbi Zalman Schachter-Shalomi (1924-2014), a Hasidic master famed for his work with Judaism and interreligious dialogue.

'Reb Zalman,' as he is generally known, was a practitioner of Hasidism, a mystical sect of Judaism originating in 18th-century Eastern Europe, which began as a folk movement that popularized and made accessible the esoteric teachings of Jewish mysticism (known as Kabbalah). The movement placed a premium on heart-felt prayer, contemplation, and self-examination, while emphasizing joyful embodiment in song, dance, and holy celebration.

Like Sufism, Hasidism organized itself into various communities and lineages that followed specific teachers *(rebbe'im)*. Reb Zalman's roots lay in the Hasidic lineage of 'Chabad,' founded by the mystical genius Rabbi Shneur Zalman of Liadi (1745-1812), that continues to this day. From those roots, he went on to radically impact Judaism through 'Jewish Renewal'—a movement that sought to infuse and reawaken a vibrant spirituality in all denominations of Judaism, primarily via the teachings of Hasidism and other forms of Jewish mysticism.

So how in the world did he end up co-founding a new branch of universalist Sufism? *Oy vey*—it's complicated! For the curious, Pir Netanel has written extensively on just this question, in his book *The Merging of Two Oceans: Nine Talks on Sufism & Hasidism*. But for our purposes, suffice it to say that Reb Zalman, though a life-long devout Jew, had a deeply curious and interspiritual outlook that brought him into deep contact with a variety of religions and spiritualities, and ultimately to the one tradition outside of Judaism that he took on as his own, Inayati or universalist Sufism.

As an Inayati Sufi he was given permission to teach (by Hazrat Inayat Khan's son, Pir Vilayat), ultimately mentoring Pir Netanel for many years in a mixture of Hasidism and Sufism. In this way, our order formed and took on the name 'Maimuni'—a reference to the only known lineage of Jewish Sufis, which flourished in Egypt from about the 12th to the 15th century, and was led for many generations by the acclaimed Maimuni family, the descendants of the famed philosopher Moses Maimonides. After Reb Zalman's passing, the Inayati-Maimuni Order has continued with Sufi and Hasidic practice and study under Pir Netanel's guidance.

Unlike Sufism however, Hasidism has never had a Hazrat Inayat Khan; no one has exactly expounded a universalist Hasidism, or a Hasidism that does not inherently require a Jewish identity or the ritual practice of Judaism. We exist in a liminal space known as 'Neo-Hasidism,' a broad, loosely connected movement, of which Reb Zalman was at the forefront, to draw wisdom from and apply Hasidic spirituality outside the confines of Orthodox Judaism, tending with modern sensibilities to such issues as gender equality, ecology, and sexual orientation. Yet, even the practice of Neo-Hasidism has been almost exclusively amongst members of non-orthodox Jewish denominations, and many within our Sufi order are not Jewish at all. So though we certainly do study and practice much from Hasidism and identify as 'Hasidim,' we would not readily be recognized as such.

Nonetheless, there you have it. The Inayati-Maimunis are Neo-Hasidic Universalist Sufis. And the thinly-veiled character of 'Jami' speaks as a student of the Inayati-Maimuni order (though none but he should be blamed for his exuberant shortcomings).

But as if the hyphens weren't plentiful enough, Pir Netanel is not my only mentor, and our brand of Hasidic Sufism is not the only tradition deeply impacting the contents of this book. Before I began learning with Pir Netanel, I had already been training with my first spiritual guide, a close friend of Pir Netanel's and a student of Reb Zalman, Zvi Ish-Shalom, in his burgeoning Kedumah teachings; and for much of the period the poems herein were composed, I was engaged extensively with them both.

Now, remember I said no one has exactly expounded a 'Universal Hasidism'? Well, outside of Reb Zalman and Pir Netanel who together have forged something of that ilk, Zvi is the one person, as far as I know, who has provided a sustained context for seekers to directly access Hasidic spirituality outside of Judaism as an organized religion. However, to be sure, in doing this, Zvi has deemphasized the Hasidic or kabbalistic nature of his teachings, and does not identify them as 'Hasidic,' for numerous reasons.[3] Nonetheless, Zvi's Kedumah teachings are most directly informed by Hasidism and the larger Jewish mystical tradition in which it partakes, *and* remain wholly unbound to a particular religion.

The mentorship of Zvi and Pir Netanel in their respective environments has been the guiding influence on my adult spiritual development. Unlike the challenges faced by those attempting to practice in multiple traditions that practically conflict with each other, internally synthesizing their two teachings has been eased by notable similarities between them. Most importantly, both are universalist in orientation, that is non-exclusive and open to authentic wisdom from any source. But moreover, they share roots or connections to Hasidism.

All this longwindedness to say that this poetry springs from my heart, in which the waters of their transmissions have mixed, and gushed up as some third thing, which both is and is not representative of the original Kedumah and Inayati-Maimuni inputs 'in their purity.' Like the classic Sufi treatise on 'the metaphysics of love,' the Persian *Lama'at* (the Divine Flashes) of Fakhruddin 'Iraqi (1213-1289)—the Sufi poetic work most directly inspiring this one—many of these compositions were written almost as 'notes.'

As the story goes, every day after leaving his teacher Qunawi's lecture, 'Iraqi would write a mixture of prose and verse, which ultimately became the *Lama'at*.[4] Likewise, the poems in this volume represent flowerings from my own study and practice. They attempt to express, through the peculiarities of my syntax and embodied experience, the teachings in which I have been immersed, and the states of being and flashes of clarity I have encountered along the path.

Though I cannot claim to be a tenth—nay, a hundredth—of the poet or the Sufi 'Iraqi is, this book's relationship to Zvi and Pir Netanel is analogous to the *Lama'at's* relationship to 'Iraqi's teacher, Qunawi. It is a dish I've created with the ingredients left to me by my teachers; though I've burned it clumsily, I hope you'll find it nourishing, even if not gourmet.

Now that you know something of this work's location, its container, I would like to speak more directly to its contents. As it is situated inside traditions that have existed, in some cases, for thousands of years, providing anything close to a comprehensive overview of the source material with which it is in dialogue would be impossible. Thus, I hope to merely introduce the aspects most salient for this work in particular.

Before continuing however, we must address an elephant in the room. As a keen reader, you may have noticed the absence thus far of a critical word—*God*. This was intentional, as I did not want to begin using it without qualification. But it does indeed deserve special attention because, as with all Sufi poetry, God is *the* subject at hand. But the word 'God' looms so large, and is far too often weaponized or otherwise distorted. So if you are not fond of the word or idea as you are familiar with it, allow me to echo the olive branch once extended by Reb Zalman to his Buddhist friend: "The God *you* don't believe in, *I* don't believe in either."[5]

God, as we see it, is not a thing requiring belief in its existence; God is not a *noun*, not some old white guy in the sky, but a *verb*, the transcendent ground and immanent, perpetual motion of the universe. To get a better sense of this, let us look at the two core names of God in Sufism and Hasidism. In Sufism, as in Islam, the central name of God is the Arabic *Allah*, which simply translates to 'God,' or '*the* God.' And in Hasidism, as in Judaism, it is the unverbalized four-letter holy name, *yud-hey-vav-hey* or *YHVH*, a placeholder for the ineffable divine being, which English bibles mostly translate as 'LORD.'

Dissecting these words, as Sufis and Hasidim alike love to do, proves revealing. As Pir Netanel writes: "The great Sufi master Najm ad-Din Kubra (1145-1221) points out . . . *Allah* is made up of four letters—'*alif-lam-lam-ha.*' The '*alif* and the first *lam* are the definite article in Arabic, *al*- or 'the.' But when you put two of the same letter together in Arabic, as we have with *lam-lam*, it signals an intensification of meaning related to what follows. In this case, the aspirated *ha*, which is symbolic of and sounds like the breath as we exhale it, *ha-a-a-h*. Thus, *Allah* is '*The very breath*,' the subtle essence that pervades and connects all being!"[6] And as Zvi teaches: "The name *YHVH*, the four-lettered name of God . . . is simply the past, present and future tenses of the [Hebrew] word 'to be' expressed in a verbal construct; *HYH* means was, *HVH* means is, and *YHYH* means will be . . . *YHVH* is the totality of all that ever is, was, and will be."[7]

Thus, when speaking of God, this is the sense I typically have in mind: God as the universe, the totality of being, the very breath of life. But this is just the tip of the iceberg. In Islam and Judaism, and thus Sufism and Hasidism, each of these core names are surrounded by a vast constellation of other names, designating God's, or reality's, qualities and attributes (compassion, wisdom, strength, etc.). For instance, Sufis use a list of 99 such names known as the *asma al-husna,* the 'most beautiful names.' For though all these traditions believe above all else in the unity of God, the unity of all being, that unity is not simplistic—within the one is the many. God plays all parts, but it's not that parts don't exist.

From this perspective, the nature of reality is recognized as 'radically non-dual,' meaning: reality is a unity containing infinite diversity that in no way separates or undermines the underlying unity. Said another way: however many beings and objects there may be, in however many dimensions, worlds, or multiverses, all of it logically exists as an ever greater whole, a single universe. Thus, the anthropomorphic or otherwise symbolic God-language used within the traditions can be understood as speaking to various facets of reality; because if God is the Totality of Being, all that was-is-will-be, the various facets of God are aspects or qualities of the infinite existence in which we find ourselves.

This universe is *alive, interconnected, responsive.* As a butterfly flapping its wings causes a tsunami halfway across the globe, a human's heartfelt intention ripples across the cosmos. That's what we're really talking about here—not merely the 'nature of reality,' but how one interacts with this living unity with its diversity of forces and beings. What is the process of coming into right relationship with the universe, i.e. God?

What is some of the territory, the pitfalls and states of being, one might encounter along the way?

And this brings us back to the aforementioned 13th-century Persian Sufi classic, the *Lama'at (Divine Flashes)* of Fakhruddin 'Iraqi. For in speaking to this dynamic of universal relationship (the universe relating to itself and us to it), I merge the two streams of the Inayati-Maimuni order and the Kedumah teachings (those of Pir Netanel Miles-Yépez and Zvi-Ish Shalom respectively), similarly to the way 'Iraqi merged the two streams flowing through him to create the unique charm of the *Divine Flashes*.

See, 'Iraqi's teacher, Sadr ad-Din Qunawi, was the close student of the Andalusian Sufi master Muhyiddun Ibn Arabi (1165-1240), generally recognized as Sufism's greatest philosopher. But 'Iraqi had a dual-transmission, and prior to studying with Qunawi had spent many years under the tutelage of Shaykh Baha'uddin Zakariyya Multani, who had inherited the teachings of Ahmad Ghazzali and his 'school of love.'[8] Thus, 'Iraqi's *Lama'at* combines the teachings of Ibn Arabi and Ahmad Ghazzali (Qunawi and Multani), by juxtaposing prose and verse, essentially giving the same teaching in the language of philosophy (Ibn Arabi) and then in poetry (Ghazzali).

Those two streams in many ways mirror those of Zvi and Pir Netanel, and a core element of each is shared between this work and 'Iraqi's. These two elements of the teachings of Ghazzali and Ibn Arabi, as reflected in the teachings of Pir Netanel and Zvi, constitute two of the major Sufi ideas woven into Jami's poetic language and my own spiritual life.

The first element is the core metaphor of Ghazzali, that of 'Love, Lover, and Beloved.' Through the language of Persian love poetry, Ghazzali articulates the spiritual path in terms of the lover (the human aspirant) in relationship with the Beloved (God). But it's not that simple.

The language of love poetry employed by Ghazzali and 'Iraqi isn't incidental or merely a metaphor for union and separation with the divine; it is also just human love poetry—humans loving other humans. For as Hazrat Inayat-Khan notes: "Sufism is the religion of the heart, a religion in which the most important thing is to seek God in the heart of humanity."[9] Hence, the lines between human and divine love become intentionally blurred in the radical Sufi teachings on love. Deciphering who the lover, beloved, and 'I' represent is part of the game, and it always changes and/or operates at multiple levels simultaneously.

Nonetheless, absolute unity underlies all these teachings, and that unity is the Love—that which transcends and includes the lover and the Beloved. Moreover, as 'Iraqi says: "Beloved, love, and lover—three-in-one."[10] In the mystic mirror, Ghazzali and 'Iraqi see the dynamic interplay of lover and beloved as part and parcel of 'God's self-manifestation,' the endless unfoldment of a singular universe.

It is this non-dual conception of love that sees loving divinity and loving creation as inextricably linked, which serves as a central axis in the teachings of Pir Netanel and the Inayati-Maimuni Order. It is he who introduced me to Ghazzali, 'Iraqi, and this radical 'school of love' (not to mention everything else as it relates to Sufism). And even more than the teachings themselves, Pir Netanel has served as an embodied exemplar of this 'path of love.'

To unpack the other element that this work integrates from 'Iraqi's *Divine Flashes* (that which mirrors a core element of Ibn Arabi's philosophy), we must introduce something critical to this whole discussion, and shared between the teachings of Zvi and Pir Netanel.

Given the radical non-dual nature of reality/God, human beings are not only *not separate* from the totality. No, it is much grander than that: as each of our cells contains the DNA of our entire body, so each particular manifestation contains the totality. An individual simultaneously contains and affects the whole, and is contained and affected *by* the whole. Simply put, all the mystical traditions we've been speaking of recognize reality as a fractal—an endless pattern that is self-similar at any and all scales, in which any part of the pattern displays its entirety.

Here we arrive at an essential question for a spiritual seeker: if we recognize ourselves as being divine, a microcosm 'made in the image of God,' how do we actually manifest that divine potential, given we typically experience our surroundings and ourselves, and thus act, for lack of a better term, 'not-divinely'?

It is in addressing this question for myself where the teachings of Ibn Arabi come into play, through the medium of Zvi's Kedumah teaching. Though the language and cultural context differ in significant ways between the formulations of Ibn Arabi and Zvi, they both hold the following general view. Because God is the Totality of Being, reality is inherently comprised of God's 'Beingness,' 'Presence,' or 'Light,' that as noted earlier is fractal in nature. The essential structure of the human being thus parallels that of the cosmos. And what is that structure on a fundamental level? The divine qualities, names, and attributes.

To use a classic example: if we envision God's being as light, white light represents the full spectrum of light together, the absolute singularity of God and the universe. But when 'God creates the world,' when the one becomes many, *à la* the Big Bang, that singular light refracts into the now particularized colors of the light spectrum. Those colors signify the divine qualities and attributes, which Islam, Judaism, and their respective mystical traditions refer to through the constellation of divine names mentioned previously, most of which are found in or derived from the Qu'ran and TaNaKh (or Hebrew Bible).

Thus, as we are microcosms of the whole, those same divine qualities are the essential building blocks of our experience, our bodies, minds, souls, etc. Returning to the question with which we began this excursion: if this is true, why are we so often personally and collectively acting 'not-divinely,' out of alignment with our true nature? The general answer from this perspective is that the 'lights of being' are manifesting in a distorted manner, the real divine qualities occluded by gross approximations, the pure quality of strength, for example, manifesting as a distorted will to dominate one's fellow. This is where we approach the heart of the matter, the practical implications of this heady cosmology.

From this view, we actualize our divine potential by integrating and clarifying, developing and awakening, the spectrum of divine qualities. As our embodied experience partakes in God's continuous self-manifestation, this process does not consist of abstract grasping, but attuning to the unique revelation coming through our very bodies, minds, and hearts, *in this very moment.* In the language of Ibn Arabi, one who embodies the divine qualities masterfully, having had their personhood transmuted in the Being of God, is recognized as an *Insan al-Kamil* (a Perfectly Complete Person).

While the Sufi 'school of love' in which Pir Netanel participates, tends to encode this metaphysical concept in the language of love and poetry, this same idea of the divine qualities, names, and attributes is central there as well. For instance, 'Iraqi says, "Love tailors the lover in a cloak of radiance and perfection, adorning them with the accoutrements of exquisite grace [i.e the divine qualities]: the lover looks at themselves and sees only the color of the Beloved . . ."[11] And similarly, when explicating the above concept of God's qualities and their role in human transformation, the lens of love-lover-beloved is commonly employed.

Critical to this discussion of integrating the divine qualities is the idea of *fana* (annihilation) and *baqa* (subsistence), which is Sufism's language for the idea, found in traditions the world-over, of spiritual death and rebirth. Generally speaking, the human approximations of the divine qualities reified in our personality structures are so radically distant from the 'pure qualities of God' that experientially, one must be 'annihilated' to be reborn and 'subsist' on the light of God, the pure qualities, rather than the 'false lights of the ego-self (*nafs*).' As one Sufi poet clearly states: "A mystic is one who passes away. They abide in the essence of that which is real. Such a person is pure, clear wine without dregs. Now whole, they display the Most Beautiful Names [the *asma al-husna*, signifying the attributes or qualities of God/the universe]."[12]

This poet's use of 'wine' as metaphor suggests another trope of Sufi poetry worth unpacking, for the many symbols offered by it have become commonplace. To decode some of these briefly: the 'wine' is love; the 'wine-giver,' God or the Beloved; 'the drunkard' signifies the seeker or lover intoxicated with God's Presence; 'the cup' or 'world-displaying cup' represents the heart as the center of one's perception and consciousness, and a reflection of the entire cosmos; and 'the tavern' symbolizes the ground of Sufi training, a Sufi gathering house (a *khaniqah* or *tekke*), or more broadly, the 'arena of life.' However, to be sure, the drinking of wine has generally been strictly metaphorical; almost none of these Sufis actually drank alcohol, as most were deeply pious Muslims in Islamic societies which forbade it.

With all that said, we have covered some of the aspects of Sufism and Hasidism most directly informing the poems to follow, such as the concept of God *(Allah* and *Y-H-V-H)*, the radically non-dual, fractal nature of reality and the human being, the idea of God's qualities as reflected in humanity, and the language of wine and love. Though we have only just scratched the surface of these traditions, and truly more basics are missing than are present, the aspects highlighted are those that feel most consequential to the work in question. Other core themes and symbols, such as the imagery of seed and tree, fire and ash, have been left unaddressed; as even though Sufi or Hasidic inputs have influenced them, they feel clear enough in the context of any particular poem.

Throughout the book, however, I make many technical references not covered here, relating to different Sufi and Hasidic concepts, but also to a broad array of other influences, most notably other religious or spiritual traditions. Thus, I have sought to make these more accessible by including longform endnotes. Some explain fairly obvious references— names, quotations, foreign terms, etc.—and some address references that may not be so obvious, but seem significant or in need of clarifying. Throughout the notes, special attention is paid to the particular Hasidic and Sufi inputs belonging to the Kedumah teaching, and to a greater extent, the Inayati-Maimuni lineage.

Despite trying to provide enough background to situate this work in its proper context as Sufi poetry (and more specifically but laboriously, as Neo-Hasidic universalist Sufi poetry in the lineages of Zvi Ish-Shalom and Pir Netanel Miles-Yépez), space and my own limitations have thwarted any sense of thoroughness in this endeavor. But as

I, a mediocre representative, have prattled on about these mystical traditions, I have offered the curious reader an appendix of recommended books that can serve as further reading on these subjects.

While these poems are ladened with traditional content, *stylistically* they aren't very 'traditional' at all (unless it be in their wild, mystical tone, complete with third-person self-references). The classic Sufi poets wrote in Persian or Arabic, among other languages, in the poetic forms popular within their respective cultures, such as the four-line *rubai* or couplet-based *ghazal*. But as an American English-speaking hippie in the 21st-century, I have been raised on modern free verse, and even more so on hip-hop and spoken word. Thus I embrace these as my native forms.

More than a page poet, I am first and foremost a spoken word artist and rapper, and all the poems herein were conceived as oral pieces of art. Hence, they are not really meant to be read, but rather spoken, even if mentally, with a strong sense of cadence and rhythm. Consequently, I have tried to use punctuation and line breaks, among other techniques, to convey the poem's flow. Nevertheless, you will not read them as I would; so I invite you to make them your own, to find your rhythm inside theirs.

Though not written systematically, upon reviewing this collection I noticed numerous throughlines, and decided to shape the random fragments into four parts, tracking a certain trajectory of 'the lover.' Included are various illustrations from Edmund Sullivan, made for Edward Fitzgerald's 1859 English translation of Omar Khayyam's *The Rubaiyat*, which went a long way in popularizing Sufi poetry in the West.

Having provided this context, which to me feels both too much and too little, I must ask your forgiveness. I said I wanted to speak *with* you about spirit, and here I've gone on and just talked *at* you about particular spiritualities, rather than the workings of spirit itself.

Nevertheless, I was being earnest earlier: I do want to speak with you, *not at you*, about love and divinity and all the rest. As I see it, in your reading of a poem, you will be 'speaking,' as your heart and mind and soul interact with it. For the meaning of art is not autocratically dictated by the artist, but co-created between the artist, viewer, and art itself. Despite these poems springing from my personal vantage point, I hope you find them resonant, and we can compose some epic music together.

By the time this reaches you, the ink on my side will be dry, but I invite you to keep adding to the holy discussion. As the great 'Sufi' Bruce Lee said: "Research your own experience; absorb what is useful, reject what is useless, and add what is essentially your own."[13]

Come, join the choir of mystic misfits.
Let us hum some merry hymns
and sing some tragic songs.

NOTES TO THE INTRODUCTION

1. The second and third definitions given are traditional sayings with no exact source, while the first and last definitions are respectively from Pir Netanel Miles-Yépez and the Bektashi Order.

2. "We believe in Allah and what has been revealed to us and what was revealed to Abraham, Ishmael, Isaac, Jacob, and his descendants; and what was given to Moses, Jesus, and other prophets from their Lord—*we make no distinction between any of them*, and to Him we fully submit." (Qur'an 3:84)

3. See the appendix "Kedumah and Judaism" in Zvi Ish-Shalom's *The Kedumah Experience: the Primordial Torah*.

4. See, *Fakhruddin 'Iraqi: Divine Flashes (Classics of Western Spirituality)*, tr. W. Chittick and P. Wilson, 45-46

5. The Buddhist friend in question was Chogyam Trungpa Rinpoche (1939-87). And as I have heard it recounted many a time by Pir Netanel, this response came with laughter, after Trungpa's young son asked his father, 'Is there a really a God?' and Trungpa slyly looked directly at Reb Zalman and said, 'No.'

6. *The Teahouse of Experience: Nine Talks on the Path of Sufism*, Pir Netanel Miles-Yépez, 60

7. *The Kedumah Experience: the Primordial Torah*, 53

8. *Fakhruddin 'Iraqi: Divine Flashes*, 33-62

9. *Religious Gathekas*, Hazrat Inayat-Khan, #1

10. *Fakhruddin 'Iraqi: Divine Flashes*, 76

11. Gender-neutral rendering of *Fakhruddin 'Iraqi: Divine Flashes*, 84

12. Binawa Badakhshani in *Love's Alchemy: Poems from the Sufi Tradition*, tr. David and Sabrineh Fideler, 171

13. *Striking Thoughts: Bruce Lee's Wisdom for Daily Living*, Bruce Lee, ed. John Little, 176

PART I

THE WARNING

*What I wish
they would have started with*

A Flash of Fangs Before Dawn

After three days of waiting at the door,
the aspirant's told:

Should you walk the path?
At this point . . . I don't know

Do you have a choice?
If so, run away—as far as you can go

If you don't, well then, friend:
that's your cross right there,
if you want it, pick it up,
it's yours to bear

Don't believe hagiographies—
they show pearls while hiding
the friction which made them

Spirituality's not endless bliss!

Feeling the world tear itself apart,
slap you in the face
without raising a hand to retaliate
is a terrible, terrible burden

The gilded cup shimmers,
but its wine tastes
only of bitter medicine

Its drinkers cry from hoarse throats:
'My God! Why have you forsaken me!?'

A violent death awaits those
who dare to cross the boundary,
traversing the gate of
fiery angels and flaming swords
surrounding the tree

Look at me,
a wretched sore on society's heel—
you don't wanna end up like Jami

Go get rich, or better yet,
be happy and loved

Leave the impossible task
for the foolish ones . . .

And if still you should be compelled
to jump down, and follow the lovers
to the bottom of the well

Don't get tripped up
by all this talk of unity
and non-duality

All dualistic and relative
truths still exist

God's totalizing dominion, the fact that
'all's in the hands of heaven,'
doesn't negate personal responsibility

The path requires choosing wisely,
operating impeccably morally

A great master once
denied cause and effect,
so reincarnated as a fox
for five hundred lives

Don't fall for faulty conclusions,
and fall from your exalted station

When they show the secret,
hold your tongue

You're surrounded by spears;
there's no ground to stand on

You're precariously
human and divine,
simultaneously

Saying, 'I am the Truth,' is only
true from one perspective,
and in terms of action,
it's generally not helpful

So I'm hesitant, but what am I to do?
Not exclaim the truth of your brilliance?!

How can I stop writing
odes for the lovely one,
when Her beauty
so demands them?

Part II
The Rise

*When one finds themselves
a facet of the holographic One*

*When one finds their Beloved
not only in their soul,
but the soul of all others*

*Where Her overwhelming
beauty and grandeur
transforms and invigorates the lover*

*Where all Her many-hued threads
weave the beautiful diversity
of the universal tapestry*

THE WHEEL OF TIME

A thousand civilizations tumble,
and a thousand more prophets
sprout from the rubble

the Alpha—the Omega
the wheel of time always wins

Its course cyclical
its force centrifugal,
scattering souls
to the edge of existence

Yet it's also centripetal,
courting souls
into the blackhole
of the Singular

Fruitful Darkness

I bow to this fruitful darkness,
typically silent, archetypal artist

Calm before the storm hits:
a single breath then cosmogenesis,
effulgence unfolding par excellence

Cells cloning genetic coding,
form forming in the mist,
a blink and its missed

Existence crept in with the wind:
all of a sudden it is and was,
will be 'til long after we're dust

Taste that moment it birthed us,
lurched us from eternal slumber

That perfectly still ground down under,
undergirding the universe's journey

A shroud to seek refuge through

Broken then poof—born anew
after a dip in the healing pool

It swaddles and swallows you,
effacement makes fresh face possible

CLEAR FLAGON, NO FLAGON

Proposals of Preparedness:

How big—how porous—is your container?

Can light shine through
those self-structures?

How much can you surrender?

Go down
        down
                down

Under the surface,
where seedlings
make their dirt bed

We can never know
the unknowable essence—
isn't that obvious?

We're seeing our own reflection,
hearing our own vibration echoing

yet God is the Generous Maker,
forever replicating fundamental patterns

so She's endowed us,
with the fullness of Her bounty

All has already been given, gifted

Your soul: a rubik's cube
its solving: the unlocking of treasures

And see how every second,
Presence connects pieces of the puzzle,
completing the picture, through endless
transformations and transmutations

She seeks out your inner chambers,
Her names forsaken, buried in mud

Cries for Her children,
Her qualities dormant inside you
to rise from their slumber

The cup colors the water:
can your cup be Totality?

Not by trying,
but by allowing

See how silly it is—
trying to get something
that's already been given?

By allowing- by listening- by attuning
to Her Beauty, manifesting in and as
our body-soul space, we attune
to everchanging grace

Each second a new fancy-
how whimsical Her dancing-
stepping- twirling- following the leader

Love follows you,
and you follow Her

The shape of your vessel
shapes Her blessing;
but Her wine grooves
the contours of your flagon

Lōōk, Lōōk
Clear Flagon-No Flagon
All Wine
Magic!

DRINKING THE OVERFLOW

Heart overflows with effulgence,
gushing, rushing

What to do with this
luminescent water,
surging, spilling over,
soaking the orchard,
transfiguring the skin?

Hands in air,
Who knows?
Speechless,
Look—it's everywhere

Her face bursts forth
from every face and form;
what to do but be
in Her Presence?

Leave thoughts for philosophers

Leave me with my love,
to play and pray
to share this precious space

Goodness gracious,
goodness is so gracious

She gives and gives and gives . . .
amazing

Her well never dries up!

Each instant fresh and original,
never replicable, infinitely special

Literally each moment- each form
each action- each soul
utterly unique

You never cross
the same river twice,
and neither does God!

What is distance,
what is nearness,
when You are my essence?!

What ridiculous concepts!

the All was always One
multiplicity in reality—nonexistent

His essence, Her attributes
completely singular—frictionless

My God speaks of Herself,
through our mouths
which is Her mouth,
how plain and profound

God—the Holy, Indivisible, Totality of Truth

How sweet Her kisses,
How luscious Her lips

How orgasmic this commingling
of absence and presence!

She's everywhere- i'm nowhere-
she's nowhere- I'm everywhere-
all the lines are blurred

No—lines never were

More jealous
than any other lover,
She won't even permit
the existence of any 'other'

What exquisite grapes She's grown,
plucking the weeds,
tenderly watering
Her friends' vineyards

Jami sprawls out,
eating merrily, drinking wine
in bed with his girlfriend

"L'chaim"

BABA

Baba,

"God is beautiful and loves beauty"

You are beautiful, and I love beauty

We're a perfect match!

The Sheepskin Throne

Your everflowing chalice
drips nectar to realms below,
golden threads descend
into the crevasse

A fleeting path of dust,
in the ray of light squeezing
through the keyhole

Grab hold of it—*follow it home*

Stolen away to other worlds, peeking in
on points of time, coordinates of space

Their words flow through
you like gentle waves,
whispers loudly reverberate

The continuum folds in on itself,
erasing distance

This Now comprised of chambers,
each holding,
in an eternal, living snapshot,
a moment

The sage sits on a
blue sheepskin throne,
gazes into past and future,
communing with souls
both old and yet to come

The illuminated masters gather,
huddled together,
hearts mirroring each other

Infinite repetitions of the Holy Name,
self-similar permutations,
one the Majestic, one the Knower,
another the Beautiful

The chorus magnetizes your spark:
truth seeking truth for truth's sake

The One Being digests the individual,
spurting out diamonds,
indestructible light-bodies

Totality Point

Time s t r e t c h e s,
fits more than its share inside itself

Totality collapsed into a point-
a dot- a speck .

Its faint glimmer grows bigger,
grows brighter,
its rays peeking
over the mountain

Sun extending,
sprawling out at dawn,
dancing- sparkling- tickling insides

Dredging up our sparks in exile,
saplings seeking water,
swamps longing for rivers
flowing over waterfalls

Endless, dimensionless
nowhere, everywhere,
it's utterly confounding

Jami stares jaw-dropped,
awestruck in love

LIFE AS ART

Waiting for flowers
to bloom through steel,
for the ethereal to become physical,
the material to become divinized

Crystalizing inspiration,
lightning trapped
in a glass bottle

That microsecond flash
extended beyond itself

Temporal yet eternal reverberations

Descending, layer by layer
from subtle to gross,
ascending, from gross to subtle

Collapsing ladder forms circles,
hierarchy deconstructed

Ethereal spirit/physical material
interpenetrated

Creating Creation—Created Creator,
In the Made, the Power of the Maker

That moment—
when endless, amorphous space
erupted everything all at once,
with a Big Bang, a thundering AUM,
when ??? said, "Let there be light!"

That moment
gets replicated endlessly,
a blueprint for
pandora's box of possibilities

Tiny moments/creatures
reflecting the creative principle

Life in all its facets,
the most fundamental
and exalted art form

The Tabernacle

Build a sanctuary
for the divine to dwell

Beam by beam,
socket by socket,
breath by breath

Following the roadmap,
the travel notes,
of the sacred architect,
the spirit of guidance

Build a sanctuary—
where pleasure's made an offering,
your presence becomes a blessing,
a prayer for the world's sanctification

Winking While Wincing

Friend,

God smiles—
reaches hands into hearts,
turns the knob to turn on
the faucet of compassionate love

The radiance of Her majesty,
displayed in heroic acts of kindness

Grace tenderizes us,
melts barriers and barbed wire

Christ winks while wincing
under a crown of thorns,
knowing mind meets
empathetic wound

All the while held
in boundless mercy

God loves us sinners
more purely than I love anyone

His acts can't be fathomed

We are just learning the Way,
that way that the Lord's sheep
have been shown and walked before

The trusted path
of prayer and goodness,
faith and daring

God is my one true love,
in whom all my loves exist

As Solomon said:
"I am my beloved's
and my beloved is mine"
(Song of Songs 6:3)

Lost & Found in Love

Love once kissed me,
with such force I forgot myself

Surprising me, suddenly,
we were in bed

No coy chase,
just a single, silent, bold
"I want you"

She brought me inside her,
and there, lost in rapture,
having forgotten myself,
some mysterious object

Dripping rainbow diamond,
no, smooth warm obsidian,
ah, bubbling purple geyser

Form after form, so fast
I saw with a cosmic eye

This form was no form,
but the form of forms,
containing all, bound by none

And this was the very essence
of my lover- the essence of my self

Having forgotten myself in Her,
I found myself in Her, as Her
being my truest peculiar self

The Selfish Lover's Conundrum

My love's forbidden, unrequited,
risking sanction- censure- rejection

Only a madman would
engage this endeavor,
but indeed—mad I am

I'd sell my home
for a lock of her hair,
trade my life and limb
for a glance of hers
in my direction

The whole town knows this well,
hears me wailing as much
through the dead of night

Feet bloody, voice raspy,
roaming in search of her

I think I found her shadow
in the form of my soul-spark:
"Jami, Jami, is that you?"

Wait, wait, am I looking for her,
or looking for me?

It's all gotten very *tricky*

GOD'S BODY

Her face: a beaming sun

Her hat: that revolving ring of moons

Her eyes: supraconscious supernovas
cutting through illusion

Her heart: this galactic cluster,
swirling architectonic web,
self-communicating
channels of vibration

Her belly: the celestial womb,
fountain of Being,
gestating the Point of Life
that reveals the point of life

All is Her play, Her canvas,
Her portrait, Her colors,
filling the space She
forms and surrounds

Revealing new marks of beauty
with each second's turning

Jami found his soul-root,
nestled in the freckle
below Her right eye

How delightful!

MUSTARD FLOWERS

Mustard flowers blooming,
faces wrapped
in yellow shawls beaming

A seedling seeing its tree-being,
feeding on waves of the wind,
fragrance of lilacs perfuming the air

Even honking's an oddly
satisfying inclusion
in the synesthetic cacophony—
as if the world texted: *"don't forget me"*

Like a buoy we just rock
with the ebb and flow,
nothing to do—nowhere to go

Everywhere you are
is where you need to be,
all that arises was destined to be

Floating in that cavern suspended
between infinitely distant poles,
space stretches smoothly—
without friction, filling every direction

Resting as the body of cosmic light,
sitting in that space
between Mahadeva's brows,
vision piercing veils of separation

Pausing for brunch with
Nizamuddin's beloved Amir

Mycelium strands of liquid luminosity
continually branching outwards

Master the path,
and the goal arrives
of its own accord

The Force

Please don't force it,
the force don't take
kindly to coercion

It only ever follows the model
molded at the origin,
forged in the molten core

There's no *shirk*- no partnership-
no other of course

All things can accord,
'cause all things are the one thing
in their ultimate source

There's nowhere to abort

Surrounded, confounded,
and washed up on shore,
he's muttering crazy utterrings
about the Lord

Heroic Drunkards

A flower for the followers of fragrance,
journeyers through celestial spheres

The holy swaying chorus-
assemblies of raucous blazing hearts-
the bush that won't burn up

Humming home
a constant blur of motion,
seeking turning returning
ever still burning

Servants of a higher cause,
the wellsprings swell and overflow,
their gushing fills the reservoirs

Saturates the lovers-
heavy happy drunkards

Spun around the sun of One,
who dances with Her minstrels

Those heroes who have run from home,
staff in hand, cloak and bag

They cannot eat, cannot sleep
this love has made them mad—
ravished all they thought they had

My lover is a jealous one,
She's come to reclaim all Her Land

COME & SNIFF THE PRESENCE

Come and sniff the presence,
its roses blooming
beauty and its message

We are this magnificence—
there's no existential question

The guide shines a light
for mysterious steppin

Like dreams that
merge within themselves,
souls inhabit different shells,
get grumpy- rusty- crusty-
like a crustacean's does

But that spark's always
hiding in the dark—
scratching at the surface

It tastes like passion
spiked with purpose

I swear these purple orchids,
speak in light-beams with the trees
and are always cordial

I slip and slide inside
and out of portals,
consult the soul
and nevermind the oracle

See pure lands
where all the land is fertile,
palaces erupt from every kernel,
Jedis fly by and there's
saints in every corner,
miracles down every corridor

There's no sortin' out—
the whole assortment perfect

A Jigsaw Jig

Love spirals like a wave:
its tube existing for just one-
short- glorious moment

Riders ride 'til the ride ends,
exhilaration—bodies entwined in space

That dance that's like that wave—
just one short glorious moment

A snapshot- a crystal-
enshrined in collective memory,
each thread tied to the other

Interlocking hoops,
Black Elk decodes the pattern,
the immaculate, geometrical
underpinning of manifestation

Each traveler's piercing of the veil
opens the way

Like a pickax chipping away
at dense rocks of obscuration,
a sword pledged to the Holy One
and Her messianic experimentation

Still—Dogen enters
the abode of enlightenment,
and all sentient things
enter alongside him

What an inexplicable
intersecting jigsaw jig:

A single star starts
tapping its feet,
and the whole night sky
begins to twinkle

COSMIC DRAMA

We bring the everywhere and always
into the here and now

Cosmic dramas reenacted,
through these fleshy,
multi-dimensional starship suits

God gives birth to the universe,
like mind gives birth to words—
say 'Hooray' for fractal-babies!

Unscripted Story

God's glory: an unfolding story
enacted by us—the actors

Through your eyes
the divine sees itself,
knows what it means to be itself

Self-reflexivity:
the power of divine self-recognition

In a world corroded by vacuousness,
this the only explanation:
humanity an integral part
of God's continuing explication

The unfurling of swirling cosmic lights,
reflected in human's bright mirror image

Microcosms living, fulfilling
the macrocosmic, undefined,
and not-yet-realized vision

Disregard dogmatic doctrines
of being predestined

Though all that will ever be
existent is already present,
the universe lives unscripted—
an impenetrable mystery

All who know are really
steeped in not-knowing

Before their softened eyes
all reveals itself,
like a lover undressing
slowly and playfully

Always fresh, completely original,
the cosmos expose themselves,
arising *ex-nihilo*, born fresh
each micro-moment

The enigmatic movement
between subtle and gross,
only known by those
who trace the flower
to the dirt from which it grows

Walking happens,
but no one walks this lonely path

The road which ends unexpected,
at a cliff whose edge extends
to the bottomless pit
of the fathomless abyss

Where narratives begin and end
but no words are said

* A Most Lively Enlivening Death *

Jesus Christ!
Christ never died, look inside

You're beckoned into the presence
and blessedness of unending light

Reclamation of your proclaimed birthright:
unimpeded sight and everlasting life

A star amidst night, likened to God
'cause you're literally made of Her

Absolutely everything,
made of the same inexorable libido,
call it Shakti or lala-poppy-groppy
it changes nothing

We're constantly running from a truth,
which by its nature displays itself
right in front of our faces,
with each amazing facet of creation

How solid we feel behind our hard cases!
How mired we are in expired mindsets!

Let this very breath
extend endlessly . . .
dissolving into vast space

Then rest in this,
rapidly still, loudly silent,
exquisitely majestic resonance—
for His sake
and all Her children's

Human & Divine

Singularity split into
ten million itty-bitty pieces,
mirror shards reflecting Indra's net

The whole space-time continuum,
projected across worlds
and precariously parallel realities

The potential of a planted seed,
made manifest in fruits on the tree

Dances of cosmic breathing:

He inhales—
the universe ceases to exist,
annihilated in His might and glory

She exhales—
voila, the myriad things arise again,
nourished by wise compassion

Frolicking in divine love and splendor,
we're always being breathed

This death and resurrection
of mind and reality
happens inside us constantly

We are the totality in actuality,
no abstraction,
not some fanciful flight of imagination

Everything spirals in on itself—God contracts,
concentrating into particularization

The four worlds become singular,
rendering hierarchy obsolete

Midnight flights to the heavens
through sinew and bone,
blood and muscle

All the angels could hide in your heart,
and still it would not be crowded

Unbound, infinite in possibility,
harmoniously co-existing,
with the whole as the whole

This morning I became an undead
wrathfully compassionate deity-mage,
riding crystalline shapeshifting lightships

It all feels normal—
coffee and news
and strolls as usual

Mysticism made earthy,
practical, human,
no dimensions excluded,
just more included

Our whole being
through and through revealed,
every level precious and beautiful

Ongoing explorations
keep yielding wondrous results—
reality: no less mysterious as ever

Consciousness goes through
all types of wonky transformations

Light shines from end to end
and the seer sees eternity,
then forgets, goes back to 'normal,'
i.e. dull, boring, obscured

No judgements,
ahhhhhhh remembering

'There's that soul-piece I lost;
I've been looking for that.'

It feels right to be who we are,
and wrong to be who we're not—
who'd have figured?

We are it all,
eating our cake
and having it too

Individual and cosmic,
human and divine,
perfect and fallible

An Ancient Song

This an ancient song sung before

Woven in the stories,
engraved on the bones
that became dirt long ago

Its humming still fills the biome,
bound in networks of mycelium cords

Ten thousand cultures
have come and gone

But their heartbeat
keeps beating in the ground,
sprouting in the sunflower,
swiveling its head searching for light

The song sticks wherever it lands:
on the next messenger

Rendered
in a thousand and one tongues,
remixed and sung
in a million plus

You know the one—
it goes 'ba-ba ba-ba ba-ba bum'

Like your pulse.
Like the electrical force of volts.
Like Earth's inner core.
Like rain pitter-patters on the floor.

We've always
joined in with our voices,
anything and everything
to make music with

Feet and drums,
sticks, bells, computers,
a whole assortment
of quirky instruments

Priestesses sing it to invoke
the turning of every age

Sailors sing it to calm the waves

Workers whistle its rhythm
to pass the day

This that earth song,
heavens song,
human song

Peculiar translations, renditions,
varying rates of oscillation
of the vibration
of unconditional love

The Fountain

Spinning circuitry,
pulsating electromagnetic fields
spraying, spewing particles

Essence separates itself
from its dust cloak,
shakes off all traces of otherness

Returns you to yourself,
your source and your breath

The whole spectrum
traversed in an instant,
blistering blinding flashes
knocked backward—off-axis

Carpet ripped from underneath
your tapping feet

Thrust upward/downward
spun around

Directionality's all funky

Standing at the crossroads
of a thousand paths

Stumped. * shrug *

*"I don't know,
here sounds fine,
no need to move"*

Enveloped in sinking quicksand,
smothered in honey or kisses
or some ambiguous sweetness

It's so meaningful and meaningless

The insect's flapping wings
express the holy message,
and worlds crumble
over and over in every second

Soul as silly-putty,
stretched and played with,
recycled endlessly,
evolving through transmigrations

I died ninety-nine times
as I penned this testament,
each out-breath
a refreshment from death's lips

The fountain keeps erupting,
then tumbling,
and rushing forth once again

Love & Knowledge Dialogue

Knowledge said:

Without wisdom, one drowns
in the sea's choppy waters;
with it, one can ride
the waves effectively

As one must have a boat
to safely traverse the ocean,
so by God's grace one must
fortify one's body-soul,
to safely navigate this
illusionary world

To which Love replied:

Imagine a drop that
extricates from the ocean,
then has the audacity
to try and build a ship
to escape itself

Stop running my friend!

Puncture your boat,
let your droplet reunite
with the rest of your body

The only life worth living
is one drowned
in the depths of love

And with that,
the captain's heart cracked
and he jumped off the deck

And the boat of knowledge
smashed against the reef

Sinking in the giddy,
passionate embrace
of the undulating love-sea

Part III

The Fall

Where all the wounds become exposed,
all the metaphysics feel vacuous

Where Her Presence manifests
as gaping, glaring Absence

When the seeker stops seeking,
subjugated, compelled to surrender

When the lover's matured,
even empowered, by Her bitter herbs

God was like:
"Cool you got it,
now try it upside down
with your hands tied
behind your back."

When the ground bottoms out
and the supports crumble

Freefall . . .

Love P
      L
      U
      N
      G
      E
      S
    hurtling
into the abyss

A seed implanting itself
in your innermost heart,
hiding itself from your vision

How wonderful it once was:
gazing at Her grace-full play
for hours through the night

How infatuated I once was
(you know how the young are
when freshly in love)

But the heart's shining star
falls forth to earth as a seed
to fulfill its destiny—
becoming a luminous tree

Hidden, it lies dormant,
no effervescent pep in the step

Body heavy, marble statue

Her fragrance sunk
into my ragged robes

This deadened skin
absorbed (or quashed)
the living light

I no longer notice her perfume,
nor feel the soft brush
of Her skin against mine

But under these stone bones,
some subterranean stirring,
the star-seed preparing its sprouting

Love's hibernating

Who knows how
She'll emerge next spring,
what fruit She'll offer
when the time is ripe

A House In Ruins

Love returned
with torturous despair

A fortune traded
for a sip of her glance

This house left in ruins

Every cell saturated
with the pain of longing,
pierced by distance

Thirst which knows
not of quenched—
dry burning aching,
the heart's writhing

Layla!

Why must you
drive Majnun mad?!

THE ENDLESS ROAD

O pathless path,
meandering, winding way
across the desert,
toward the one

I've sold my possessions,
for the honor to walk
behind these poor fellows

Turning back,
I see nothing but a sandstorm,
erasing our fresh tracks

I remember the cliff
I almost fell from,
the one you jumped from—
and shutter

Wrap woolen shawl tighter,
pressing on
against the whipping wind

THIRSTY

Love was a raging fire,
now ash is all that remains
of my funeral pyre

No flames, no play,
no rising towards heaven,
just gray gloomy days
for your broken brethren

Chasing after that taste
that lingered for a while,
leaving a depleted, fleeting
memory of her smile

But try as I may,
I'm stalking the gazelle in vain

I've wandered 'round the labyrinth,
doubling, tripling backwards

Still—no sign

Rugged as sandpaper,
my mouth's dry

"Mamma! Mamma!
Dov'é l'acqua?"

"Mother! Father!
Where is it!?
I need water!"

THE DESERT PRAYS FOR RAIN

I have solemnly seen,
the beauty of a leafless-
withered- winter tree

Let this sunken soul
know sweet sweet
flourishing spring

New leaves, new wings,
new breath to breathe

May arid desert
be luscious forest,
bring rain to this
parched explorer,
glorious glorious
God given water pouring

I would drink the nectar
if only I could manifest
some sense of Her

Or glance at her reflection projected
through the lens of Her messengers

These bees struggle to find pollen

This shell empty
like a centuries-old mollusk

Grant me peace, please
bring bounty in Your nearness

Self-concern,
let alone asking for assurance,
is a weakness

But please God—
please show me you hear this

Abandon Your Self
For a Self that Includes God

Run down to the riverbank
bearing the flag of pain

Your broken heart as armor,
your humbled pride a guardian

Drink from these waters of love,
nourish that blossoming heart,
'for the night is dark and full of terrors'

Lost, bewildered,
you wander 'round the forest,
tigers pouncing from every side

You've grown cold,
enslaved to your every whim

Throw off your chains,
cut all the tethers

Abandon your self
for a self that includes God

Feel how great a distance
stands between a narrow identity,
and the perfect harmony
of creation's orchestra

You're a water-warped guitar
with a few missing strings

And my instrument's
in still worse condition

Let us cry out together
and join the holy band,
surely someone there can fix us

Or at least, we can sit in the back
as secret sinners sneaking in
to glimpse the saints

And maybe- just maybe-
we'll get one small taste

IDOL WORSHIP

Ugh!
look at us—hypocrites
inflated self-proclaimed monotheists

Crack us open,
surely you'll find idols,
the self and its vanities
worshipped in our hearts

I pray to God
to pray to God
for God alone

Spun

Soul tornado,
rapid downward whirlpool,
full-force vortex,
rung out on rocks,
power-washed inside out,
rush of a dam breaking,
electric storm collision,
supercharged river surge—
something's moving inside me

Some centripetal force
pulling me into its centrifuge

Where I'm then spun around
like water in a bucket—
just fast enough
that my mind won't fall o
                        u
                         t
Who did that?
        What is this?

What might like dynamite
awakened in the pillar?

Goddess with a thousand faces,
I long for just a second of stillness,
let's rest.

Pulling me tighter,
pushing her hips into mine,
she whispers:

"Just one more song,
one more song"

There's always another
irresistible rhythm,
another outfit to try on

She's so vivacious,
her vibrancy vexes me,
mr. frumpy grumpy man

'Babe, I'm tired—no exhausted,
thoroughly wiped out,
call me for another round
after a hundred year nap'

'You're cuter when you're happy'
she laughs,
stamping a wet kiss
on my bruised cheek

'Oy, oy, ok, ok'

She coaxes me away
from the cliff of death,
holding my shirt
edging me backward

I'm not convinced
I wanna live just yet,
but I sure as hell
don't wanna die

PHONE THE FRIEND

Sometimes,
I write love letters
to the lovely one

Or just hop in bed,
and cuddle up silently
against her warm skin

But other times,
I turn to my friend
and say:

"God!!! What the fuck?!
Where am I? Where are you?
I'm so lost, please help!!!"

And sometimes
that works too

GRANDIOSITY TOPPLED

Grandiosity toppled
by tragedy/comedy

Commonly humbled,
head ducked and huddled

Grumbling overcome
by the coming of clarity

Fair when its seen
and it's tearing the dream
of the meagerly beast—
the me we decreed
had keys to the kingdom of peace

But it seems he's a thief,
a liar, false messiah

Who mired ya, blinded ya,
chin checked ya for change
on an island of fire and mud

Siphoned ya soul,
then dropped ya
with a thunderous thud

Left in the muck,
tryna resolve
the unsolvable crux

Discover the power
endowed to crowds of cells,

surrendering together
to the ever-present endless self

The One and Only, Holy Holy
weaver of creatures and stories

Destroying cocoons
and subsuming the crude you,
whose pride is a lie,
denying the infinite light's right
to permeate life

The light cries: *"He and I cannot occupy
the same mind, place, or time"*

My ego the barrier
impairing the divine wine,
from climbing inside this rusted goblet,
preventing the giving of my whole
to the Whole to gobble it

This problematic, crassly emphatic mayor
trying to place the president
on their payroll

Crazed insubordination
of hierarchical configurations

Bastardization of the ultimate when
disowning relative, onerous limits

Attempts to mix oil and water,
negate the Creator,
displace the operation of karma

Bringing stars to Earth's surface,
herky-jerky wrenching
with purported power

Its cowardly malware,
a terrible parable of insurrection,
filled with meddling menace,
void of proper penance

Pens who neglect to give paper credit,
a calf that forgets the cow who fed it

A Taste of Ash

All I feel is *piercing*.

All I taste is *ash*.

God!

Please rectify this bloody mess,
give purpose to this sack of flesh!

WOUND UP & WOUNDED

Searing wound—
the armor I build
to protect against it

What a ridiculous cycle:
creating self-inflicted pain
to evade underlying pain

It sounds insane,
at least a bit inefficient,
like three traffic-riddled lefts
instead of a quick right

Wallowing in the plight of it,
the light—I've lost sight of it

Exiled—Presence denial

God wants to help,
but I won't let Her:
"Leave me here in my misery,
I'm not worthy of redemption."

But it's all I want

I ordered the plate,
then threw it back
in the waiter's face

Now not only maimed,
but ashamed

Countenance covered in ash—
this can't keep going, I won't last

The structure's wound up
so tightly, it's frightening

I might be strong enough to break it,
but don't know
if I have the strength to face it

A Brief Indulgence of Despair

Showers can't clean this stained soul

Inside: fear, regrets, dismay

Outside: Where do I start?

When did God's kingdom
get so dingy?

ACCOUNTABILITY

The guardian angel got drunk
and left his post,
came back to a solemn note:
"The dove fled, the queen's been dethroned."

No, no, Jami,
you left your post,
you triggered the avalanche
that crashed
and led to your remorse

THE PATH OF BLAME

My God has freed me
of good reputation

My name's already
been dishonored

Good, let me work peacefully,
in costume, away from scrutiny

In private with my Lord,
my Friend, my Beloved

May God judge me
with an eye of mercy

And may I only ever bow
to God's power

Don't Bite, But Know How to Bark

This my secret sword,
I stole it from Iblis himself

Snuck by a hundred demon-guards
For a chance to snatch it

Now that it's mine,
I'll never let it go

The whole world could attack me,
And a single swoop of my blade
Would repel them all

This self-knowledge sword sharp—
You can't gaslight someone who's sure

Go ahead, try, come at me—
I'm <u>unshakeable</u>

GOD MIGHT SNATCH YOUR NECKLACE

I'm not a sorcerer,
but I showed Leonardo
where the portals were

In the tangent curve—
swerve right

Right into a flower of life—
swept up
in winds of divine might

Like love just cut through,
a thief and a cutthroat,
She'll steal everything from you

THE CAVE OF SHADOW

I know what I'm saying
sounds illogical

I'm asking you to walk
into a pitch black cave
where shadow monsters
will disembowel you

But what did you think
all this love had to love?

We want blood and guts,
not physical martyrs but

The innermost parts
of the innermost part,
where saints and sinners
dance with arms interlocked

GOD-WRESTLING

Don't talk to me of
realization and its sweetness—
I know only this cross
and its bitterness

"Blessed are the meek"
is merely appeasement

Be **bold**,
your survival depends on it

Surrender to God—
but not without a fight;
if you get knocked out,
so be it

For lovers know of
nothing worth loving
that's not worth fighting for

God, as 'the Pure Light,'
wrathfully annihilates
all that is other than Her,
reabsorbs all into Herself

But to be human is to cradle
that terrifying grandeur,
bringing forth, coaxing out
God's supreme quality:
'Unconditional Love'

Turning light into love
is the human heart's
role in the universe,
the heart helping to pump
the love sustaining the cosmos

And in this role, the soul
which sits in the heart,
has been authorized
to challenge the Lord

As a good queen
chooses advisors who
question her honestly

Thus we enter the ring,
fight with all that blocks
the flow of mercy,
the gushing of grace

When the Pure Light flashes
wrath and destruction
seeking to destroy impurity
(see, Sodom and Gomorrah)
the lover of goodness,
of humanity, of Earth, of all beings
seeks mercy- *demands* mercy

Sometimes they're defeated,
the mudslide of karma
proving unstoppable

But sometimes they triumph:
find a backdoor in a back alley,
to flip the switch
which unlocks the font
of tender compassion,
triggering the alchemical process,
turning lightning into a cozy fire,
the Light into Love

Those who know
don't say 'all is equal,'
they bind God's left hand
and massage Her right,
seeking to be shielded
from Her by Her

Praying in the name of
the Merciful, the Compassionate,
they say: "I seek refuge
with the Lord of daybreak,
from the evil of what He created,
from the evil of the dark night
when it penetrates" (Q: 113:1-2)

Longing

This longing
a curving tunnel
whose end I'll never find

I want all of Her
and She is infinite;
how could I not
keep scrambling after Her?

She is sand between my fingers

I say: sleep in, stay in bed awhile

And yet she's off,
before the morning light
sneaks by the window

With heaviness I sigh,
the sound a heart makes
breaking under strain

My God!
Why must you be so coy?

Have you not sown,
in the soil of these souls,
the secret seed
entrusted to humanity?

Why leave people
in rags scrapping to eat,

when you made them to be,
queens amongst queens
in the ranks of the One?

You promised to be with us
in joy and tribulation,
so Levi Yitzhak's suing
over breach of contract

Where are You
when the lonely call?

Papa, you withhold our inheritance,
you have no legal right!

I cry for what is ours
but was lost,
ripped from our shaky grasp
by primordial shatterings

Running down
the tunnel of longing,
yelling for my love's attention

Wishing to magnetize Her,
with the poignant beauty
of a pitiful panged heart

Wanting to know Her
in all her ways,
wanting to know the impossible

Still, frenetically setting forth,
searching in all directions

Stretching toward territory unchartered,
chasing Her through every world

This heart a maniac,
wanting what she can't have

Writing verses in rose petals,
along cobbled streets
to attract Her glance

Everyone in the city
has heard the poems

And although no one
has ever seen Her,
we all rave of Her Beauty
and long to meet Her

A Hoarse Hallelujah

a cracked heart, a twisted soul
a restless dream of a lover lost
abandonment rekindled
body remembers

the hollow feeling
the hundred needles pricking
the sputtering floundering
the pit it turned into
the lions den I live within

a ghoulish existence
a haunting gauntness
a ravenous skeleton
walking, falling . . .

black abyss
another mistress
listless drowning
crowned a shithead
implicit hypocrite
wretched imposter
still praying . . .

repentance soothes
refound value
circumstance defied
alive again

a fresh breath caress
succulent nourishment
sap fills crevasses

fortifying mortar
an eagle in Mordor

God's untouched goodness
the only triumph

a hoarse hallelujah
a stumbling finish
a bloody gold medal
a chipped tooth smile

bitterly earned rest

Nonexistence Extinguished
in the Existent

I saw the fire
and fled from my self

Face smeared with ashes

Wrapped in a cloak of oblivion
in this world and the next

Contraction & Expansion

Wear a scarlet letter, a yellow star
two inches from my center

Feel it creepin in,
my heart begins to wither

Invaded by the bitter,
shunned like the runt of the litter,
succumbing to malevolent whispers

Paint doomsday on a Tuesday
down by an excuse of a river

This mystical turned pitiful
in the flip of a scripture

An abysmal attempt,
a raspy, crass hymn,
pining for deliverance
and heavenly street-cred

Seek peace, but only see
rampaging fiery red

Eat anger, digest it,
stoke flames in my head,
communicate with ancestors
like they were never dead

Hearin hums like tidal waves
the way they descend

Extinguished in an instant,
then reemerging again,
a mildly less shitty
friend to my friend

Scuba diving in space for a bit,
breakin' out of tamed
and encased for a sec'

Just a glimpse out the dream

Looks like all is She,
no me, you, or we

It's just this unity or trinity—
nevermind all I find
in my mind's eye's
an empty infinity

THE GREMLINS

For fifty moons I've howled
with the gremlins in the graveyard—
smoking, laughing, joking with them

My friends just want to attend
the lovely beloved's birthday fest

They're rowdy, out with the crowd,
breaking bottles at the palace's edge,
clinging to the coat of royalty—
a scheme of subterfuge for sneaking by

Yes, they need to be trained,
but you can learn
from their wily ways

Integrate, integrate,
bring fractured fragments
back into the fold,
the esctatic organism
of the dancing Lord

JUICING

Suffering's like fruit
being juiced

It takes a lot of suffering
to squeeze out
a little maturation

P.S.

Don't beat yourself up,
God loves you

But She's making mimosas,
and you so happen
to be an orange

P.P.S.

I know, I know,
that's no help in a hellhole—
but still, for what it's worth . . .

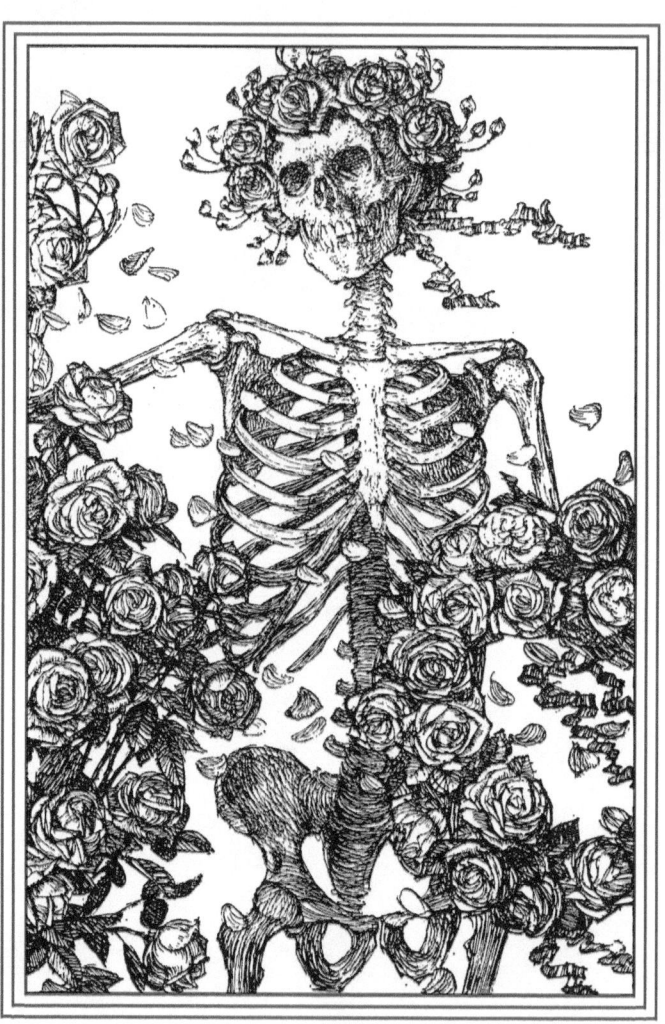

PART IV

THE RETURN

*Where rest is found
in the transcending and including of
longing, union, and separation*

*When states, stations, and attributes
become an integral holistic spectrum*

*Where love, lover, and Beloved
become one in the Real*

*When one can honestly say:
There is no God!
Nevertheless, God is!*

REDEDICATION

Amid the wreck's debris
we found a sea-kissed bottle

* cork pop *

Inside- scraps of yellowed paper,
sketches of gaunt ghosts,
scribbled by shaking hands
of our trepid, tepid younger-selves

Fears stuffed in a decaying container

A collection of rotting fruit,
attracts flies at the mishmash altar

I am running for my life,
from a villain I cannot see,
in a dream projected hazily
on the back of my eyelids

Mid-chase,
I decide I can fly,
that flying is obvious,
and I am in the stratosphere

Tracing circles round the center,
blooming like a fresh flower of life

Like the last billion years
of cell multiplication
was all leading to this

For this miracle—
for these microscopic molecules
to have configured
into stem and leaf and petal

So that some strange creature
might glance through
their perception box—
view this confluence
of phenomena

Name it flower,
see it as yellow,
smell it as delightful

Tumble through its form
into the formless One

Recognize that One as that flower,
that flower as ourselves,
ourselves as a form
of that formless One

The sacred moment envelops
the ghosts- the fears- the villains
of our haunted minds

Wraps oozing wounds with
bandages of exquisite tenderness

Gives calluses,
makes cold concrete
soft beneath weary feet

Forges stoic steel bars,
wrapping them in
warm, friendly wool

Reattached, tethered,
we return to the destruction

Begin cleaning, restoring,
sweeping away the wreckage

Lighting candles,
rededicating the temple,
sacralizing what was defamed

Everything already crumbled.
We're just here to make mosaics
with the scrap heaps,
grab rusted remnants,
craft elephant legs
for a steampunk Dali exhibit

Nestled under shrubs
atop a cobbled wall,
crumbling, cascading stones

We smoked a pipe like Sherlock's,
saw how far
our throat-singing could echo

Threw a smooth pebble off the ledge:
it skipped across the water,
went around the universe,
smacked me in the head

The compass makes no sense—
I've encompassed all things

Returned to my own life,
like a mother returns
to soothe an enraged baby

Tears of a scarred phoenix,
balm to the lesion

My future-self coaxing its present
into becoming itself

Re-Turning, Re-Membering

Courting mercy,
drawing it down by flirting
with a flurry of service

Composing the sad song
of a distant servant

Look for the north star,
with the western wind
rushing in—storming

Clarity once so clear,
disoriented and distorted

Searching for the lost door
'til the first rays of morning

Then coming to and mourning,
the destruction that was wrought
on these bones so burdened

Sure,
you lost your sorcery

You were sort of pure,
albeit not thoroughly

Went astray
from the straight path—
~ swerved ~
stumbled on the steep curve

Spoke foolishly
in front of Majesty

Now
shhhhhh
all is She

You are just as illusory
as all partners
attributed to Her Being

He is your walking
your hearing
your seeing
your talking
your feeling
your breathing

This the source of your power,
the core of your meaning

'Yours' is a misnomer,
just the best word
when speaking

This is not your body or mind,
but the temple of the heart

So renew your commitment,
and commit to renewal

Take joy in the song
of again and again
we come up short

But again and again
toward God we turn

'Cause when we return,
our Beloved is waiting,
with that for which
our heart burns

Lay & Stay

I don't know
where things will go

All I know
is when I'm with you,
it feels like home

I need no guarantees,
my love is given free

But please,
don't send me away

Here,
with my head on your lap,
I wish to lay and stay

I'll reenter the world,
for your sake
and your sake alone

But please,
don't send me away

Here,
with my hand holding yours,
I wish to lay and stay

Vacant Fireworks

Sapphire eyes
witness staff turn to snake
and a bush on fire

He said:
'Let me take off these shoes
and turn away from this place'

Tallis of light shrouding his face,
spinning jackhammer
carving inner space

Diving into depths
of the vast dark ocean

Where drunk monkeys
bang cymbals
in realms of chaos

Body shaking, *merkavah* turning,
nuclear heart fusion

Blasted back to the origin point . . .

Swallowed.

She devours us,
melts us down to essence

Refining copper to gold,
as immutable substance
undergoes endless changes

A pillar of night, sparkling
with specks of starlight

This utter emptiness:
the vessel for Her flourishing

A marriage of space and substance:
the ebb and flow of the river
within its bank

The dervish spins 'round the nail,
its unmoving nature
supporting the whirling

Her flashes remain unseen,
overpowered, obscured by the light
of clouded awareness

Then Being covers
the light of consciousness,
with the darkness of mind's
inherent emptiness

Vacant—fireworks begin,
rainbow-colored explosions
of essential play

Your games aren't Her games;
yet Her games are your play

You can't hold her:
She forever dances
without a partner

No one can keep up
with a beauty like that!

We just form circles,
bowing and cheering
as She enters and dazzles us

I turned away from the fire,
toward the gate of returning

Finding *Ani* to be *Ayin* (I to be Nothing),
Her blaze forming shadows
in the cave's secret chamber

This amalgam of iridescent stars
existing as a wish in Her heart

GODS OF BELIEF

I built a vast exquisite shrine
to the God of my belief:
crystal halls, towering statues,
ornate frescos, countless candles

There I served and exalted 'God,'
dancing in the wonder of myth

Then Truth came as a raging fire,
burning that elaborate house down

Turning my world all around,
my belief into disbelief

Shattered- groundless- bewildered-
I knew not, and yet . . .

An undeniable taste

In the tasting
came an unwitting gnosis,
intimacy with the pearl-clad princess

When knowledge became incarnate,
I once again believed—
but not as I once did

LIKE FINDING 20 BUCKS
IN YOUR POCKET

Glops of cosmic matter
squished together,
soul-juice squeezed out,
pressed with impressions

You're taught the whole truth,
then an angel comes
wipes knowledge away,
with a press of their finger
at your philtrum

Everything is forgotten,
but not lost

There's that ringing
if you listen real close,
like a distant call home

Some taste of resonance,
the sheer thrill of vibrating
with your own core

That unconditioned/unconditional
love that makes and sustains you
(also known as 'God')

Some seed starts sprouting
and we get all squirmy,
vines growing, wrapping us tighter,
wringing out confusion

Deluded self screaming,
"Don't kill me!"

Lightwaves keep crashing,
wearing down, smoothing out
our stubborn rocks,
"Relax, we're not here to hurt you."

Trees bear fruit,
some substantiality displaces
* ever so gently *
the vacuity of mental constructs

Replacing that core
structure of personhood
with the divine manner

Knowing nothing, feeling so full,
big belly Buddhas laugh,
while running and returning

States & Phases

I'm fascinated with various
states and phases:

How soul becomes solid
finds homeostasis

How mind becomes liquid
slips from its cages

How bodies turn gaseous
float to their maker

Philosophy Turned Mushy

There I was contemplating
a profound abstraction:
the nature of reality

Pondering Tantra, Vedanta, Chabad,
the world as real, as illusory,
as both or neither

And in the midst of this
mental diagram drawing,
the static got turned way up,
mind went fuzzy

Philosophy turned mushy,
felt terribly distant,
inconsequential, inadequate,
in the face of some simple, sparkling smile

There, in Presence
thought stood bewildered—
no questions, no answers

Scholarship Forgotten

I thought myself smart
surrounded by books,
quotations pressed
upon my furrowed brow

But alas,
I've forgotten all the teachings,
and am all the wiser for it

Wiser because I know I know,
and know I know nothing at all

Mmmm . . .
how free I feel to frolic as a fool!

The Masterful Actor's
Garb of Virtue

An egotist donning
the shawl of humility

I'm hoping its dye might
stain this narcissistic skin

> I mean,
> what's the difference between
> a saint and a phony,
> but masterful, actor
> who never breaks character?

> As for me,
> I'm mediocre,
> always forgetting lines,
> taking off the costume,
> letting this silly self-important ego
> romp and rampage for a bit

The question still stands, but
I've come to something akin to,
although not technically, an answer
(albeit only a personal one):

A saint, I cannot be;
I'm a sinner and accept
inevitable decrepit ineptitude

So, you—you lovely actor
so gallantly striding in that
beautiful borrowed bejeweled
garb of glorious virtues—
it is you I hope to emulate

Instructions to the Vegetable

The chef came to check
but the stew's not done

With a little salt,
a little heat, a lot of time,
the dish'll be delicious—trust us

Yes, even you too broccoli-head

Fear not, the chef's world class,
the finest there is

She'll bring out flavors in us
we never knew existed

GROWING UP

The master smiles at the folly
of so-called adults, us children
clinging to narcissism's naivete

'When will they realize
they are nothing
and God is everything!?'

The Razor's Edge

Living on the razor's edge,
rapid fire feedback loops
keep us on point

A second off, a lifetime missed—
the Presence be exacting

Total accuracy
or the pain starts shooting

We rode lightning,
were blinded
by its ferocious blaze

A cloud of arrows
flies through muggy air,
descends then disintegrates
in a forcefield of truth

The one who knows their own being,
knows the whole Being,
and knows themselves as whole

Souls on fire,
heart-punctured rapture,
unending desire for the Lovely One

Come, come if you're willing to travel

If you'll leave your home
for the open road

If you'll leave all that is
other than God

'Other than God?
How could it be so?
God is everything,
all that is, was, will be!'

Uh-huh yup, but
what is other than God?
What we relate to
as other than God

Where is She?
Where we let Her in

And when She wants to
charge and barge in,
there's no stopping it

She gathers parts scattered
'cross far corners of the multiverse

Dissolves them in the cauldron:
fire boiling water,
roasting lead and cinnabar
til dragons lay with tigers

She wreaks havoc 'til victorious—
when will you surrender?

Ascend to Descend

Associate with nothing;
cut any tentacle attached
to anything but God

Even your beloved teacher
should not be in your heart
at the hour of prayer

Repeating 'God, God, God,'
until experientially,
nothing exists but
the reality of God Alone

Yet, if love of God does not result
in lovingly serving Her creatures,
the beautiful people, rocks, and trees,
it's at best just a pretty heart,
with no blood to animate it

Have vitality.
Make it juicy.

Squeeze, suck, slurp
the fruit off the pit,
the pulp out the peel

Nourish the seeds,
plant them tenderly

Make God real through
your treatment of creation

But the key's this little 'me'
can't ever love properly—
no ego doesn't work for itself,
the antithesis of love

Only when I deconstruct everything,
'you,' 'me,' even the reality of 'God,'
does God become a reality for me

Only in that magic moment,
when as a newborn our eyes open
to the world born anew

Does the sanctity of everything
become blatantly obvious

And truly, it is in the inherent
sanctity of relationship
that all good virtue lies

Ascending without then descending—
pathologically vacuous

Descending without first ascending—
impossible

A Secret Treasure

I was a secret treasure
that longed to be known,
so was sown
in the seeker's breast,
as the goal of their noble quest

Seeking and finding,
losing and repeating,
each lap discovering
new meaning- perspectives-
objectives- subjective expressions

With each stroke of the pen
they add to the message

With each dish a new scent:
come taste and know
that God is good

For I speak in your peculiar tongue,
in the prayer niche of your heart,
in that secret ark
where the jewel's enshrined

I am the Mother,
all-embracing arms
smothering my loved ones,
cuddling the munchkins

Come and see the wonder:
I fit the whole universe
in your tummy

The Outer Gates,
The Inner Sanctum

At the outer gates,
it's proper to kick and scream,
in attempts to capture
the guards' attention

But once they've answered,
asked for the passwords,
opened what was barred,
led you to the Queen's steps

Shhhhhhhh
sit in Her Presence,
humble and watchful,
and if you should speak,
a simple whisper shall suffice

There, in the inner sanctum,
a drop in the cup
makes waves in the ocean

At the See-Saw's Center

Hope and fear
are as two seats on a see-saw

Only by standing in the middle,
can you avoid
being thrown up and down

There, in that center point,
we can float,
held in the oceanic womb

Suspended in the eternal
outpouring of the Now,
between absolute and relative identity

LISTEN: LOVE SINGS WITH EVERYTHING

Sometimes my soul sings like Adele:

"There's a fire starting in my heart,
reaching a fever pitch
it's bringing me out the dark"

And God chimes in like Ashanti:

"I'm not always there when you call,
but I'm always on time,
and I gave you my all,
now baby be mine"

WHEN LOVERS GATHER

glimmers of beauty emerge,
from murky bogs of chaotic confusion

anointing oil descends,
the queen's crown drips drops,
sanctifying our common ground

life flourishes on impact,
new growth rising through dirt

eyes twinkling, hinting
at some spectacular mystery

rainbows over bomb-made dust cloud—
the poignancy of juxtaposition,
cosmic heart's ability to hold everything

cries arising from its dusty corners,
grace responds naturally,
reaches into hearts to hold my loves

swaying, humming sad holy melodies,
the tune collapsed the castle

with a panged heart,
the beloved invited us
for brunch upon the rubble

THE TWO AXES

Realizing the truth is one thing,
living it another

Realization is

V
E
R
T
I
C
A
L

aligning the spine

Integration is

H O R I Z O N T A L

opening the heart

One makes you tall, the other wide;
like a mountain be both

The two axes
balance and complete each other;
keep them sharp

What's two in the student
is one in the master

Truth and Manner, *Haqq* and *Adab*,
the signs of divine embodiment

TEMPERED CERTAINTY

Internally,
maintain the fire
of your convictions,
but temper it with
modest not-knowing

Externally,
let the waters
of humble non-judgement
douse any prideful flames,
which may blaze forth
fueled by certainty's passion

Each soul has its path,
each truth its time

Calligraphic Breath

Calligraphy of the Name
painted on the breath

Inhaling—*Allah*
Exhaling—*Hu*
Filling, Emptying

The Breath guiding you
through narrow tunnels,
like a needle
threading a pearl

LINEAGE

Their names have become
sweet on my tongue

Nectar drips down the chain,
circles through the web
of illuminated masters

Those mysterious planes
on which souls meet,
beyond narrow confines
of space-time

Where souls babble to each other,
in language too subtle
to translate to words

Looking on, one just hears them intone:

Aaauuummm

Huuuuuuuuu

Ever so gently,
the whispering of God's friends
lands, sinks in the skin,
as ethereal sound-light-rays

Like luscious morning dew,
seeping into last night's cold soil

Easy as 1,2,3

The endless emptiness: the 0

Births the unbegotten 1:
God—the Totality of Being

Who relentlessly manifests as the 2:
Yin and Yang, Shiva and Shakti dancing

Their balanced rhythm creating the 3:
Love, Harmony, and Beauty

LIKE A BEAR

Find me like a bear,
gorging himself with honey

My face, my paws, all covered with it

Sweetness drips from limbs,
into this holy earth,
holder of ancient blood and bones

Rises from the crown, blending
with the tapestry of light forms

Satisfied, yet yearning for more,
Jami stands between heaven and earth

The Master Musician improvising tunes,
through this cracked didgeridoo

Escaping Without Escaping

The world blusters,
frantic zigzag frenzying
drives us inward

Searching for that still-point—
that vista in which our gaze
can expand and e x p a n d and e x p a n d

Until it collapses
under its own vastness,
pushing us fully backward
to the womb of the origin

But what pushes us forward?

The marketplace is so distasteful,
people blurting falsities,
yelling over one another
trying to sell you something

Why shouldn't we escape it?

No, no, wrong question

How can we escape it?
Who's escaping?
What are we gonna do—
pop out the matrix!?

My God!

The same frame that received soul,
and birthed mind
(the only place of the separate 'I,'
without which we could never find
that jewel that is You)
demands involvement
in this sticky shitshow of a soul soup
(also known as human affairs)

I, the lover, fleeing the blustery world
to seek God, the Beloved
is based on a false premise—separateness

The One already decided to experience
being human in global community,
with other humans, fungi, fauna, flora,
all the Earth's forces

And that One is beautiful,
gracious, and caring

Soooooooo
without separate self's neurotic grasping,
our lives become loci for channeling
Her beauty, grace, and care
into Earth's biosphere

See,
escaping without escaping,
world disappearing then reappearing—
epistemologically reborn

SIMPLE TRUTH

Love manifests
infinite power
effortlessly

Truth is simple

There is no need
for over elaboration
or fancy articulation *

* Yes, I recognize the irony

THE RIDER, THE WITCH, AND THE WHIRLPOOL

The belly of the beast beckons

That turbulent, black, swirling whirlpool,
pool of nothingness, font of blessedness,
womb of souls, boiling cauldron
of pre-eternal matter

Bubbling in the bellows,
inscribed with the blueprint

Installed with a secret switch
to flip the poles of consciousness—
I influence everything,
everything influences me

The witch with a toothy grin,
stirs the soup knowingly,
laughing her head off

Laughs echo and echo
re-echoing endlessly,
in this silent silo,
vacuum of imperturbable space

The headless rider
serves her soup to souls silently,
his lips offered to the witch
at the price of his head

And at the night's end,
he dips into this nothingness,
this blessedness,
the cackling abyss

Disintegrated as entity,
integrated into
the cosmic liquid-crystal mesh

The rider turned henchman finally gets,
why the witch laughs off her head

Returns to serve souls
with what would be
a knowing grin

If his head wasn't
just this nothingness,
this turbulent whirlpool
that one day will take you

BUSY LOVER

Long ago I used to chase her,
slip love notes as I passed by

But now *she chases me*,
coaxing with kisses,
whispering promises of union

Alas, I'm not to be enticed
by her fleeting scent

'My love,
I can't come to bed quite yet,
I have too much work to do'

PART 1:
_____

A FLASH OF FANGS BEFORE DAWN

Feeling the world tear itself apart, slap you in the face without raising a hand to retaliate . . .

A reference to the New Testament teaching: "If anyone slaps you on the right cheek, turn to them the other cheek also. And if anyone wants to sue you and take your shirt, hand over your coat as well." (Matthew 5:39)

'My God! Why have you forsaken me!?'

The opening line of Psalm 22, and what Jesus cried out while on the cross. (Matthew 27:46)

. . . traversing the gate of flaming swords surrounding the tree

This imagery comes from the following verse: "After He [God] drove the man [Adam] out, He placed, in front of the Garden of Eden, cherubim and a flaming sword flashing back and forth to guard the way to the tree of life." (Genesis 3:24) Within the Jewish mystical tradition, 'the Tree of Life' signifies the true 'body' of God/reality, which structurally parallels human beings and the whole cosmos. Teachings on 'the Tree of Life' convey a constellation of divine qualities and layers of reality, and a 'chain of emanation' that provides a framework for how manifestation continually appears ex-nihilo, and unfolds from the subtlest to the most dense of forms.

God's totalizing dominion, the fact that 'all's in the hands of heaven'

This refers to a teaching of the Polish Hasidic master Rabbi Mordechai Yosef Leiner, the Ishbitzer Rebbe (1801-1854). Speaking to the absolute nature of divine providence, he radically recapitulates the Talmudic dictum, "Everything is in the hands of heaven [i.e. God] except for fear of heaven" (Berakhot 33b 23-25), as "Everything is in the hands of heaven, *including* the fear of heaven." (*Living Waters: the Mei HaShiloach*, tr. Betsalel Philip Edwards, *Parshat Vayeira*, 45)

A great master once denied cause and effect, so reincarnated as a fox for five hundred lifetimes

A reference to the Zen koan 'Hyakujo's Fox': ". . . [a student] asked me 'Does a person who has accomplished their practice fall into cause and effect?' I replied to him, 'One does not fall into cause and effect.' Thereupon I fell into having a wild fox's body for five hundred lives. I beg you Osho [a Zen Priest], give me a turning word now.' Hyakujo said, 'One does not evade cause and effect.' At these words, the old man attained great enlightenment." (*The Book of Equanimity*, tr. Gerry Shishin Wick, 28)

Saying, 'I am the Truth' . . .

'I am the Truth' (Ar. *Ana'l-Haqq*) was the ecstatic exclamation (*shath*) uttered by the Persian Sufi master Mansur Al-Hallaj (858-922), which infamously led, or at least contributed, to his execution.

PART II:

THE WHEEL OF TIME

the Alpha—the Omega

'The Alpha' and 'the Omega' are translations of '*al-Awwal*' (the First) and '*al-Akhir*'(the Last), two of the 'most beautiful names' (*asma ul-husna*), the ninety-nine Arabic names of God designating God's attributes, which are repeated, audibly or silently, by Sufis in the ritual practice of *zikr* (remembrance). These terms are also intentionally brought in to recall their use in English versions of the New Testament's *Book of Revelation*—"I am the Alpha and the Omega" (1:8)—which mirrors statements made in both the Qu'ran ("He is the First and the Last" 57:3) and the Hebrew Bible ("I am the first, and I am the last" Isaiah 44:6).

THE FRUITFUL DARKNESS

. . . after a dip in the healing pool

'The healing pool' is a metaphor for both the heart and the 'living waters' of the Divine Presence found therein. For example, Obadiah Maimonides (1228-1265)—a Jewish-Sufi in Egypt after whose family the Inayati-Maimuni lineage takes the latter part of its name—uses the cleansing of a pool as his metaphor for the quintessential Sufi practice of 'cleansing the mirror of the heart.' (See, *The Treatise of the Pool*, tr. Paul Fenton, 91-93). And more generally, the 'living waters' is an epithet of the Divine within the Jewish mystical tradition, denoting the feminine Divine Presence (*Shekinah*).

CLEAR FLAGON, NO FLAGON

Look, Look, Clear Flagon-No Flagon, All Wine, Magic!

A play on a typical trope of Sufi poetry—an experience of absorption in the Divine, or of 'ego-death,' is likened to a perfectly clear cup, that when filled totally with wine, seems to 'disappear.'

DRINKING THE OVERFLOW

You never cross the same river twice, and neither does God

A typical Sufi notion. As the aforementioned Fakhruddin 'Iraqi says: "He never twice shows the same face; never in two mirrors does one form appear." (*Fakhruddin 'Iraqi: Divine Flashes*, tr. W. Chittick & P. Wilson, 81)

His essence, Her attributes, completely singular—frictionless

An allusion to a common understanding, in both mystical Judaism and Sufism, that the Divine essence, which transcends any possible descriptor, and the spectrum of divine attributes (i.e. names, qualities, lights, etc.) form an absolute singularity (rather than a unity comprised of two or more parts). Using a masculine pronoun in reference to the divine essence and a feminine pronoun in reference to the divine attributes is intentionally reflective of the language conventions of the aforementioned two traditions.

More jealous than any other lover,
She won't even permit the existence of any 'other'

This line conveys one aspect of Sufism's teachings on God's 'jealousy;' as Fakhruddin 'Iraqi puts it: "So jealous is He, all others are destroyed: He must Himself act every part!" (*Fakhruddin 'Iraqi: Divine Flashes*, tr. W. Chittick & P. Wilson, 79) The concept of 'God as jealous' is not unique to Sufism— for instance, in the Hebrew Bible it states explicitly "I, Yah your God, am a jealous God" (Ex. 20:5)—but perhaps nowhere does this concept become more highly developed than in the Sufi 'school of love' (*mazhab-i 'eshq*), with its poetic use of the jealous lover motif. For instance, the school's founder, Ahmad Ghazzali (b. 1058) speaks of "three swords of jealousy (*ghayrat*) which cut the lover's attachment to anything but love," stripping away layers of identity—even that of the Beloved Herself—until only love remains. (*Mirror of Love, Meditations on the Sufi Path of Love, Book I: Inspirations*, Pir Netanel Miles-Yépez, 17)

"L'chaim"

Hebrew for 'to life.' An equivalent to the English 'Cheers,' commonly said as a toast before drinking alcohol.

BABA

Baba . . .

A broad term of endearment and respect, common across the Middle East and South Asia, literally meaning 'father,' which here refers to my *murshid* or 'spiritual guide.'

"God is beautiful and loves beauty"

A *hadith* (record or 'tradition' of the prophet Muhammad's words) commonly referred to by Sufis, for whom following beauty in pursuit of God, the Beautiful, is a core tenet of the spiritual path.

THE SHEEPSKIN THRONE

The sage sits on a blue sheepskin throne

An allusion to a custom of the Turkish Jerrahi order (*tariqa*) of Sufism: during communal ritual gatherings, the head of the order, the *pir*, sits on an elevated seat (a throne) on a sheepskin dyed blue. (See, *The Garden of Mystic Love: Volume I: The Origin and Formation of the Great Sufi Orders,* Gregory Blann, 224)

The illuminated masters gather . . .

This is inspired by the prayer *Toward the One*, used by all Sufi orders that spring forth from Hazrat Inayat Khan, the founder of universalist Sufism who wrote this prayer:

Toward the One,
the Perfection of
Love, Harmony, and Beauty,
the Only Being,
United with all the Illuminated Souls,
Who Form the Embodiment of the Master

. . . one the Majestic, one the Knower, another the Beautiful

These equate to three of the ninety-nine *asma ul-husna*, 'most beautiful names' of God: *al-Jalīl* (the Majestic), *al-Khabīr* (the Knower), and *al-Jamīl* (the Beautiful).

. . . truth seeking truth for truth's sake

A play on the traditional Hebrew saying *Torah lishmah*, 'Torah for its own sake,' which refers to a Jewish ideal of studying Torah with a pure, truth-seeking motivation. Integral to this play on words is that within the Jewish lexicon, 'Torah' does not only mean the Hebrew Bible (the Written Torah), or the extensive tradition of commentary such as the Talmud (the Oral Torah), but also 'the Truth;' and a true scholar or master of Torah is regarded as 'a living Torah scroll,' meaning 'a living embodiment of the Truth.' Thus, one could also say . . . 'Torah (the Truth embodied in human form) seeking Torah (the specific methods and guidance which serve as roadmaps to the Truth) for Torah's (the Truth's) sake.' (For a more thorough articulation of this idea, see, *The Kedumah Experience: the Primordial Torah*, Zvi Ish-Shalom, 65-67 and associated notes)

LIFE AS ART

Creating Creation—Created Creator, In the Made, the Power of the Maker

This brings together two different, but similar, ideas from Sufism and Hasidism. "The power of the Maker within the made *(ko'ah ha-po'el ba-nif'al)*" is an oft-repeated phrase in Hasidic literature. And "Creating Creation, Created Creator" alludes to the following esoteric understanding of the great Sufi metaphysician Muhyiddin Ibn 'Arabi (1165-1240): "The ocean of the Cloud is a *barzakh* [lit. isthmus] between the Real [*al-Haqq*] and creation. Within this ocean, the possible thing [i.e. a creature] becomes qualified by Knowing, Powerful, and all the divine names [i.e. the attributes of the Creator] . . . and the Real becomes qualified by wonder, receiving joyfully, laughter, rejoicing . . . and most of the attributes of engendered [i.e. created] things." (*The Sufi Path of Knowledge: Ibn al-Arabi's Metaphysics of Imagination*, tr. William C. Chittick, 181)

. . . with a Big Bang, a thundering AUM, when ??? said, "Let there be light!"

Hindu philosophy considers AUM the root syllable of the universe, the original vibration from which subsequent existence reverberated. This understanding of cosmogenesis is here equated with the Big Bang, and the verse, "And God said: 'Let there be light' and there was light." (Gen. 1:3)

THE TABERNACLE

. . . the spirit of guidance

See the note on *The illuminated masters gather . . .* (pg. 141)

THE SELFISH LOVER'S CONUNDRUM

. . . for a glance of hers in my direction

The poetic tradition of Sufism employs the 'glance of the beloved' (*kirishmah-i ma'shūqī*) and other 'features' of the beloved to describe various states and processes: "The hair, the cheek, the mole, the stature, the eyebrow, the glance, the smile, and even the rebuke of the beloved, are all signs. Each of these signs relates to a place in the lover from which a specific desire and quest (*talab*) arises." (*Mirror of Love, Meditations on the Sufi Path of Love, Book I: Inspirations*, Pir Netanel Miles-Yépez, 22) Though its meaning varies, I typically understand 'the glance of the beloved' as a kind of 'divine attention' that illuminates and exposes one.

GOD'S BODY

. . . gestating the Point of Life, which reveals the point of life

The 'Point of Life' refers to what my teacher calls the 'Point of Light,' among other names. This is his translation of the Hebrew term *'nekudah'* (lit. point), a technical term within the Jewish mystical tradition denoting the most essential layer of the individual soul—the soul-spark (*nitzotz*), the ray of God-light at the core of every soul that constitutes one's 'true self.' (See, *The Kedumah Experience: the Primordial Torah*, Zvi Ish-Shalom, 206-207 and associated notes)

. . . filling the space She forms and surrounds

This alludes to the Hasidic idea (returned to often by my teachers' teacher and co-founder of the Inayati-Maimuni lineage Rabbi Zalman Schacter-Shalomi) that God both fills (*memaleh*) and surrounds (*sovev*) the infinite existent worlds, i.e. paradoxically, God simultaneously becomes creation and remains wholly transcendent outside of the created universe. (See, *Rabbi Zalman Schachter-Shalomi: Essential Teachings*, selected and introduced by Or N. Rose and Netanel Miles-Yépez, 25)

Jami rests in his soul-root, nestled in the freckle below Her right eye

This is inspired by the renowned Kabbalist Isaac Luria of Sfat (1534-1572), whose "doctrine of the 'soul-roots' . . . posits that each soul is an intrinsic part of a larger constellation of souls that share a common root . . ." (*Radical Death: The Paradoxical Unity of Body, Soul and the Cosmos in Lurianic Kabbalah*, Zvi Ish-Shalom, 62)

MUSTARD FLOWERS

Mustard flowers blooming, faces wrapped in yellow shawls beaming

The traditional color of the Chisti-Nizami lineage of Sufism (which Hazrat Inayat-Khan, the founder of Universalist Sufism, represented) is a bright yellow, the same hue as mustard flowers. To this day, on the festival of *Basant*, devotees in New Delhi don yellow and bring an abundance of mustard flowers to the *dargah* (grave-shrine) of Nizamuddin Awliya, after whom the Nizami branch of Chishti Sufism is named. According to folklore, this custom commemorates the following event: "One day, Amir Khusrau—the famed poet, innovator of *qawwali* music, and beloved disciple of Nizamuddin Awliya—saw a group of Hindu village women dressed in yellow, carrying mustard flowers and singing on the road. Khusrau asked where they were going, and was told: 'To the temple to offer our god flowers.' Khusrau then asked whether this would make their god happy; and when they said it would, Khusrau immediately dressed up in a yellow saree, and carrying mustard flowers, went before Nizammudin Awliya singing. Recognizing his favorite disciple and amused by his costume and song, the saint, who had been sunk in a depression over the loss of his nephew, finally broke into a smile." (adapted from the article, "How Delhi's Hazrat Nizamuddin Dargah Began Celebrating Basant" Rana Safvi, *Scroll*, Feb. 12th, 2016)

. . . sitting in that space between Mahadeva's brows

Mahadeva (lit 'Great God') is an honorific title of the Hindu deity Shiva. The point between the eyebrows is connected to the *ajna chakra*, the subtle-body center popularly known as the 'third eye,' used by some Yogic traditions, such as that of Sri Shivabalayogi (1935-1994), as a key place of focus in meditation.

Pausing for brunch with Nizamuddin's beloved Amir

These two figures—Nizamuddin Awliya (1238-1325) and Amir Khusrau (1253-1325)— are a revered teacher-student pair within Chisti Sufism. For context, see the previous note from this poem on *Mustard flowers blooming . . .*

THE FORCE

There's no shirk- *no partnership-no other of course*

Shirk, an Arabic word literally meaning 'association' or 'partnership,' is a prominent and nuanced concept within Islam.

Typically, *shirk* refers to idolatry or polytheism, believing in a multiplicity of independent divine powers rather than a singular God—the ultimate theological sin in a monotheistic context. However, my use of this term relates to a more subtle, radical view commonplace amongst Sufis: not only are there not independent gods or forces, nothing but God exists.

HEROIC DRUNKARDS

. . . assemblies of raucous blazing hearts- the bush that won't burn up

Here, the 'raucous blazing hearts' *are* 'the bush that won't burn up.' This concept comes from a teaching of the founder of Eastern European Hasidism, Yisra'el ben Eliezer, the Baal Shem Tov (1698-1760). Space does not permit a full retelling, but here's the gist.

Commenting on Moses's encounter with the burning bush, the Ba'al Shem Tov teaches: "Where does the messenger of God become known? In the heart afire, which is the sincere and simple intention of the heart. And where is this 'heart of fire' to be found? In the midst of the thorn bush . . . There are fruit trees [wise scholars] . . . and there is the humble bush that bears no fruit [the humble and unlearned] . . . [Scholars] can quench their thirst with the insight they gain in study. . . [However] with their simple and sincere prayer, in their holy ignorance, they [the humble and unlearned] are the flame that is not quenched; their thirst can never be satisfied . . . So the teaching is one must never be satisfied with one's humility before God; from the higher to the lower and the lower to the higher, there is always room for repentance [*teshuvah*]." (*A Heart Afire: Stories and Teachings of the Early Hasidic Masters (Revised Edition)*, Zalman Schacter-Shalomi & Netanel Miles-Yépez, 44-53)

My lover is a jealous one, She's come to reclaim all Her Land

See the note on *More jealous than any other lover* (pg. 140).

A JIGSAW JIG

Interlocking hoops, Black Elk decodes the pattern . . .

Black Elk (1863–1950) was a medicine man of the Oglala Lakota tribe in the Great Plains region of North America, who at the age of nine had an immensely powerful vision, which laid the ground for his life's work. The imagery of him decoding a pattern of interlocking hoops stems from a small snippet of that grand vision, as recorded, presented, and embellished by his biographer: "I was standing on the highest mountain of them all, and round about me was the whole hoop of the world . . . I was seeing in a sacred manner the shapes of all things in the spirit, and the shape of all shapes as they must live together like one being. And I saw that the sacred hoop of my people was one of many hoops that made one circle, wide as daylight and as starlight, and in the center grew one mighty flowering tree to shelter all the children of one mother and one father." (*Black Elk Speaks*, John G. Neihardt, (Excelsior Editions, 2008), 33)

Still, Dogen enters the abode of enlightenment, and all sentient things enter alongside him

Dōgen Kigen (1200-1253) is a Japanese Zen master, and the founder of the Soto Zen school. The understanding conveyed in this line derives from his teaching that: "When even for a moment you sit upright in *samadhi* [meditative absorption] expressing the *buddha mudra* [the form of the buddha] in the three activities (body, speech, and thought), the whole world of phenomena becomes the *buddha mudra* and the entire sky turns into enlightenment . . . Furthermore, all beings in the world of phenomena . . . at once obtain pure body and mind, realize the state of great emancipation, and manifest the original face." (*Treasury of the True Dharma Eye: Zen Master Dogen's Shobo Genzo*, ed. Kazuaki Tanahashi, 5)

COSMIC DRAMA

We bring the everywhere and always into the here and now

The pairing of 'the everywhere and always' and 'the here and now' was frequently employed by Pir Vilayat Inayat Khan (1916-2004), a modern master of Universalist (Inayati) Sufism in America, through whom the Inayati-Maimuni Order traces their lineage. For example, speaking to the exact point above, he notes: "The new perspective is a matter of bringing the divine desire into the human will, the 'everywhere and always' into the here and now." (*Keeping in Touch*, newsletter #31)

UNSCRIPTED STORY

Humanity an integral part of God's continuing explication

That creation serves as a medium through which God can know Herself is a common understanding within Sufism. The most succinct, apropos, and widely-used Sufi expression of this comes in the form of a *hadith qudsi* (a non-Quranic statement of God recited through the prophet Muhammad): "I was a hidden treasure and I yearned, I *loved* to be known intimately. So I created the heavens and the Earth so that they may know me intimately." (Omid Safi, *Radical Love: Teachings from the Islamic Mystical Tradition*, 21)

The unfurling of swirling cosmic lights, reflected in human's bright mirror image

This alludes to a central idea within the aforementioned Ibn Arabi's metaphysics, alluded to in the introduction: the human being serves as a 'locus of manifestation' (*mazhar*) for the divine qualities (also referred to as names, attributes, and lights), which comprise the essential substance of all creation; and as they arise within an individual's consciousness, 'the mirror of one's heart' reflects these various attributes in a unique way, more or less purely depending on the 'cleanliness of one's mirror,' the clarity of one's perceptive apparatus in a given moment. (*The Sufi Path of Knowledge: Ibn al-Arabi's Metaphysics of Imagination*, William C. Chittick, 91-96)

Absolutely everything, made of the same inexorable libido, call it Shakti . . .

Representative of the feminine, immanent, and active element of the divine, the Sanskrit word '*Shakti*' generally means the 'energy of life,' or 'cosmic life-force,' and is related to as a goddess, particularly within Tantric Hindu tranditions. *Shakti* is the primal and primordial desire to bring forth and spread life, of which human bodily/sexual energy is an expression; in this sense, it can be understood as the universe's 'inexorable libido.'

HUMAN & DIVINE

. . . mirror shards reflecting Indra's net

'Indra's net' is a metaphor for the interconnected, holographic nature of reality, used pedagogically within both Hinduism and Buddhism. This 'net'—originally spoken of as covering the abode of the Vedic deity Indra— stretches infinitely in all directions, and is made entirely of jewels, each of which reflects the image of every other jewel/the net as a whole, creating an infinite fractal.

The four worlds become singular, rendering hierarchy obsolete

The map of 'four worlds' is utilized in both Sufism and Hasidism. Though both traditions recognize reality as consisting of infinite worlds or dimensions, the model of four worlds is used for speaking to various discernable layers of reality. In Sufism, the four worlds are known as: *'Ālam an-Nāsūt* (the world of humanity), *'Ālam al-Malakūt* (the world of angels), *'Ālam al-Jabarūt*, (the world of power), and *'Ālam al-Lāhūt* (the world of divinity). And in Hasidism/Kabbalah, they are known as *Olam ha-Assiyah* (the world of making), *Olam ha-Yetzirah* (the world of formation), *Olam ha-B'riyah* (the world of creation), and *Olam ha-Atzilut* (the world of divinity). One way to understand these four worlds in terms of personal experience is the explanation provided by Rabbi Zalman Schachter-Shalomi, who spoke of these four worlds as those of doing, feeling, knowing, and being. (For a thorough comparative examination of this model in Sufism and Hasidism, see *One God,*

Many Worlds: Living in the 'Four Worlds' of Hasidism and Sufism by Pir Netanel Mu'in ad-din Miles-Yépez in *One God, Many Worlds: Teachings of a Renewed Hasidism: A Festschrift in Honor of Rabbi Zalman Schachter-Shalomi, z"l)*

That these worlds 'become singular, rendering hierarchy obsolete' is a concept borrowed from my teacher Zvi Ish-Shalom. As he writes: "In this view the epistemological categories that determine the perceptual dichotomies that separate the human and divine—and the body and soul—are erased . . . the physical body, typically viewed as the essence of limitation, separation, and dualism, is here transformed into the organ of a non-hierarchical perception that allows for particulars without it implying a gradated cosmic structure that superimposes hierarchical categories of physical and spiritual. What results from this process is a radical epistemological non-dualism that recognizes that reality manifests particular and distinct forms (i.e. it encompasses both a real ontological duality and non-duality simultaneously) without it implying architectonic categories of hierarchical rank." (*Radical Death: The Paradoxical Unity of Body, Soul and the Cosmos in Lurianic Kabbalah*, Zvi Ish-Shalom, 224-5. For what this might mean practically speaking, see *The Kedumah Experience: the Primordial Torah*, Zvi Ish-Shalom, Ch.11)

All the angels could hide in your heart, and still it would not be crowded

This sentiment derives from a *hadith qudsi* (a non-Quranic statement of God recited through the prophet Muhammad) much beloved by Sufis: "Neither my heavens nor my earth can contain Me. Only the hearts of my humble, believing servants can contain Me." As the ecstatic Sufi Bayazid Bistami (804-874) exclaimed: "If the Divine Throne and all it compasses were to pass through a corner of the gnostic's heart, they would not even know it." (*Fakhruddin 'Iraqi: Divine Flashes*, tr. W. Chittick & P. Wilson, 110)

There's that soul-piece I lost . . .

I'm here influenced by Lurianic Kabbalah and its doctrine of soul transmigration (*gilgul*), which roughly posits the following: as part of a larger cosmic restoration (*tikkun*), each soul journeys to complete itself; and the soul's completion lays in re-membering its various fragmented parts, reconnecting them to their source in the cosmic body. (See the note on *Jami rests in his soul-root . . .* (pg.144). For an in-depth elaboration of the traditional view and consequent practices, see *Sleep, Death, and Rebirth: Mystical Practices of Lurianic Kabbalah* by Zvi-Ish Shalom)

ANCIENT SONG

The song sticks wherever it lands: on the next messenger

This line in particular, and the poem as a whole, reflects an influence of the Quranic concept of every people being sent a messenger: "For we surely sent amongst every people a messenger, with the command, 'Serve God, and eschew evil'." (16:36)

This the earth song, heavens song, human song

A reference to the trinity of heaven, earth, and human prevalent across Chinese religious philosophies.

PART III:

WINTER

A seed implanting itself in your innermost heart, hiding itself from your vision

The following teaching from the 'Sufi school of love' bore influence on this line: " . . . the sense of love's 'absence' continues. This is only temporary. The *love is journeying inward to seat itself in the innermost chamber of one's being.* This is one of the most difficult ideas to understand, though it may be that to which the poet alludes . . . 'When affection reaches its perfection, 'Friendship' is transformed into enmity.' " (*Mirror of Love, Meditations on the Sufi Path of Love, Book I: Inspirations*, Pir Netanel Miles-Yépez, 22)

A HOUSE IN RUINS

A fortune traded for a sip of her glance

See the note on *for a glance of hers in my direction* (pg.143).

Layla! Why must you drive Majnun mad?!

Layla and Majnun are a famed pair of unconsummated lovers, whose tragic story has evolved and spread throughout Sufism and much of the Islamic world. As is often pointed out, thematically and in terms of influence, the closest equivalent in Western culture is Shakespeare's story of *Romeo and Juliet*.

Though details vary greatly between numerous retellings, the thrust of Layla and Majnun's love story is this. Having fallen in love at a young age, circumstances bar Layla and Majnun from being together. Wildly distraught, Majnun, whose given name was Qays, wanders totally absorbed in the thought of his love Layla until the point of madness, earning him his name 'Majnun,' meaning 'crazy,' or more literally, 'jinn-possessed.' Though their demise takes on different forms, almost all versions have each of the lovers dying before reuniting; and whether reunited or not, the story always ends tragically, with Layla and Majun's love, but also the separation between them, intact.

From this story of popular culture, Sufis have long drawn inspiration, seeing within it many fitting metaphors for the path of the lover as they seek intimacy with God, the Beloved. (For a complete English translation of a classic version of this story, see *The Story of Layla & Majnun* by Nizami (tr. Rudolph Gelpke), Omega Publications)

THE ENDLESS ROAD

O pathless path, meandering, winding way across the desert, toward the one

This whole line represents a poetic translation of the word *tariqa* (Arabic for 'path,' used to designate a specific Sufi lineage and the 'mystic way' in general), which is often described in similar terms as these, in juxtaposition, though certainly not at odds, with the 'straight path,' the *shar'ia* (the religious observances of Islam).

Wrap woolen shawl tighter . . .

The earliest Sufis to be named such wore woolen cloaks. Thus since that time, woolen items have been the quintessential Sufi clothing. The name 'Sufi' even most likely has its origins in the Arabic word for 'wool' (*sūf*). (See *In the Teahouse of Experience: Nine Talks on the Path of Sufism*, Pir Netanel Miles-Yépez, 8-10)

ABANDON YOUR SELF
FOR A SELF THAT INCLUDES GOD

'for the night is dark and full of terrors'

The catchphrase of Melisandre, 'the Red Witch,' in the television program *Game of Thrones*.

IDOL WORSHIP

surely you'll find idols, the self and its vanities worshipped in our hearts

That our very self is the principle 'idol' we delusionally serve and worship is a common Sufi teaching. Thus from this view, the normative Abrahamic prohibition against idolatry suggests: one ought to be in loving, devotional service to God/the universe/all of life, rather than to one's ego.

I pray to God to pray to God for God alone

A play on the words of Chisti master Shah Kalim Allah Jahanabadi (1650-1729): "We ask God to always ask God for nothing but God!" (*Sufi Meditation and Contemplation: Timeless Wisdom from Mughal India*, tr. Scott Kugle with Carl Ernst, 32)

PHONE THE FRIEND

Or just hop in bed, and cuddle up silently
against her warm skin

In addition to the felt sense of this experience with my human beloved, I'm here inspired by the words of Bhagavan Das (b. 1945), a living American icon at the intersection of Hindu, Buddhist, and New Age spirituality: "Meditation comes. I don't sit to meditate, I sit to love. I'm hopping in bed with the Divine Mother. Let's play Ma! Let's have fun! How are you? What's going on? You've got to get really simple with it. It's like a little girl playing with dolls. Love them and kiss them, and they come alive. And when they look at you, you look back and you feel that joy and love in your heart." (*It's Here Now (Are You?): A Spiritual Memoir*, 311)

"God! What the fuck?! Where am I? Where are you? I'm so lost, please help!"

An example of the Hasidic practice of *hitbodedut* from Rebbe Nahman of Bratslav (1772-1810), which although nuanced and potentially profound is actually quite simple: one finds a secluded place, preferably in nature, and communes with God by speaking openly and honestly in one's common tongue, as one might with their partner, therapist, or closest friend.

GRANDIOSITY TOPPLED

The light cries: "He and I cannot occupy the same mind, place, or time"

This line is inspired by two short and strikingly similar stories within Hasidism and Sufism.

The Sufi story, told in Mevlana Rumi's *Masnavi*, is as follows: "A friend knocks at the door of a friend, who answers, 'Who is it?' The knocker says, 'It is I!' But the door does not open, nor is there any response. For a year, the knocker wanders, suffering in separation from the friend before returning. Hearing a knock at the door, the friend asks, 'Who is it?' The knocker answers 'You!'

154

and the door promptly opens."

And the Hasidic story is this: "A Hasid, who has been studying with the Great Maggid in Mezeritch, stops in Karlin on his journey back home. Intending to visit his elder companion, Reb Ahron of Karlin, the Hasid eagerly hurries over to Reb Ahron's house, and seeing a light in the window, knocks at the door. 'Who is it?' Certain that Reb Ahron will recognize his voice, the Hasid calls back, 'It is I!' *Silence.* He knocks again. No answer. 'Ahron? Why aren't you opening the door?' A pause. Finally, Reb Ahron booms back, 'Who dares say 'I' in the presence of God?!' Taken aback, the Hasid mutters under his breath 'I have not yet begun to learn,'" and immediately departs to return to Mezeritch.'" (Both stories adapted from *The Merging of Two Oceans: Nine Talks on Sufism & Hasidism*, Pir Netanel Miles-Yépez, 63-64)

DON'T BITE, BUT KNOW HOW TO BARK

This my secret sword, I stole it from Iblis himself . . .

"This is a reference to Shaykh Aḥmad Ghazzalī's controversial interpretation of Iblis as God's greatest lover. Iblis is the name of the archangel who was later called Shaytān, God's 'adversary.' For when God asked the angels to bow before the human being in the Qur'an, Iblis refused in arrogance and was expelled from heaven (38:71-82). But Iblis' response to God's banishment was, 'I swear by your glory,' which Shaykh Aḥmad interprets as an example of Iblis' continued loyalty to God, and the real reason for the refusal to bow before the human being, as if to say, 'How could I bow before anything but You! You alone who are worthy of reverence!' And what sustains Iblis in hell but the remembrance of the sound of God's voice saying, *'Go to hell!'* So in love with God is Iblis, that even these last terrible words are held sacred, being the last links in the chain that connect them." (*Mirror of Love Meditations on the Sufi Path of Love, Book II: Commentary* by Pir Netanel Miles-Yépez, 50)

GOD MIGHT SNATCH YOUR NECKLACE

. . . showed Leonardo where the portals were

A reference to the Renaissance polymath Leonardo Da Vinci (1452-1519). Of note here is Leonardo's fascination with sacred geometry, and the 'flower of life' in particular.

. . . flower of life

A New Age term, popularized by Drunvalo Melchizedek, for the below symbol, found in many variants across the globe:

SHADOW CAVE

But what did you think all this love had to love?

This line's inspiration lies in the following passage: "One of my psychedelic excursions had gotten off to a bad start, and I was sinking into a really satanic bummer. As I looked about me at people turning evil, shrunken, colorless, old, and weird, I suddenly thought, *'Well, What did you think it was that needed to be loved?'* And just like that, the doors opened and I was in paradise." (*The Lazy Man's Guide to Enlightenment*, Thadeus Golas, 10)

GOD-WRESTLING

"Blessed are the meek" is merely appeasement

The rejection of this quote from the Book of Matthew (5:5) is not meant to be absolute, as I recognize the wisdom in it and in the orientation to which it points. Nonetheless, in addition to the sense of 'wrestling with God,' foundational in the Jewish tradition and directly referenced later in the poem in question, the language here is influenced by Malcolm X's strong critique of Christianity. For example: "The greatest miracle Christianity has achieved in America is that the black man in white Christian hands has not grown violent. It is a miracle that 22 million black people have not risen up against their oppressors—in which they would have been justified by all moral criteria, and even by the democratic tradition! It is a miracle that a nation of black people has so fervently continued to believe in a turn-the-other-cheek and heaven-for-you-after-you-die philosophy!" (*The Autobiography of Malcolm X,* 251)

And in this role, the soul which sits in the heart, has been authorized to challenge the Lord

In the Hasidic tradition, the role of a *tzaddik* (a righteous person) as an advocate for beings in the face of harsh judgements or punishments from God forms a prominent topic. But the sentiment of this line is indeed reflected within Judaism as a whole (see the note directly below). The Talmud, the basis of Jewish practice, goes so far as to teach: "I, God, issue a decree and the *tzaddik* nullifies it." (Moed Katan 16b)

When the Pure Light flashes wrath and destruction seeking to destroy impurity (see, Sodom and Gomorrah) the lover of goodness, of humanity, of Earth, of all beings seeks mercy- demands mercy

A reference to Abraham's role in the Biblical story of Sodom and Gomorrah, which Hasidism, and Judaism in general, commonly look to for inspiration and teaching opportunities. Upon being informed of God's plan to destroy the sin-filled cities, Abraham pleads with God: "Will you sweep away the righteous with the wicked? What if there are fifty righteous people in the city? Will you really sweep it away and not spare the place for the sake of the fifty righteous people in it? Far be it from you to do such a thing—to kill the righteous with the wicked, treating the righteous and the wicked alike. Far be it from you! Will not the Judge of all the earth do right?" (Genesis 18:23-25) And 'bargaining with God' in this way, Abraham gradually whittles down the number of righteous people for whose sake Sodom and Gomorroh should be spared to ten. (Genesis 18:26-32)

they bind God's left hand and massage Her right,
seeking to be shielded from Her by Her

Hasidic teachers, following the precedent of earlier Jewish mystics, use the arms and/or hands of God as a metaphor for two of God's attributes, the left arm/hand representing the attribute of judgment, and the right that of love.

'Seeking to be shielded from Her by Her' reflects the following recorded words (*hadith*) of the Prophet Muhammad: "I seek refuge in Your pleasure from Your wrath, and in Your forgiveness from Your punishment. *I seek refuge in You from You.*" (Sunan Ibn Majah, Book 34, #15)

in the name of the Compassionate, the Merciful

A direct translation of the Arabic phrase '*Bismillah ar-Rahman ar-Rahim*' that opens all but one chapter (*surah*) of the Qur'an, and is thus used in Islam/Sufism as a traditional opening formula for prayer.

LONGING

. . . Levi Yitzhak's suing over breach of contract

Levi Yitzhak of Berditchev (1740-1809) was an early Hasidic master, and passionate defender of the people, who even had the audacity to put God on trial, inspiring this line and those surrounding it: "His daring, his frankness were drawn from his very despair. So was his revolt. For the first time a Rebbe took man's defense against his Judge . . . the Rebbe [did not] hesitate to remind God that He too had to ask forgiveness for the hardships He inflicted on His people . . . When a Jew sees *tephillin* [phylacteries] on the ground, he runs to pick them up and kisses them. Isn't it written that we are Your *tephillin?* [Brachot 6a] Are you never going to lift us toward You?" (*Souls on Fire: Portraits and Legends of Hasidic Masters*, Elie Wiesel, 107-110)

. . . primordial shatterings

A reference to the Kabbalistic concept, later integrated into Hasidic thought, of 'the breaking of the vessels' (*shevirat ha-kelim*). The basic thrust of this teaching being: as God created the world, the vessels meant to hold the light of God couldn't withstand the pure radiance and shattered, plunging the created world, which was designed to be a perfect reflection of God's light, into a state of brokenness and disarray. Thus, the mythic journey within the logos of Kabbalah/Hasidism is to heal the broken body of creation, enacting a simultaneously personal and cosmic restoration (*tikkun*).

A Hoarse Hallelujah

. . . an eagle in Mordor . . .

An homage to the ending of J.R.R. Tolkien's *Lord of the Rings* trilogy, in which giant eagles save protagonists Frodo and Sam, from a seemingly inescapable death in the darkened realm of Mordor.

Part IV:

Rededication

view this confluence of phenomena . . . a form of that formless One

This passage reflects the influence of the following lines from Jack Kerouac's *Scripture of the Golden Eternity*: "I was smelling flowers in the yard, and when I stood up I took a deep breath and the blood all rushed to my brain and I woke up dead on my back in the grass. I had apparently fainted, or died, for about sixty seconds. My neighbor saw me but he thought I had just suddenly thrown myself on the grass to enjoy the sun. During that timeless moment of unconsciousness I saw the golden eternity. I saw heaven. In it nothing had ever happened, the events of a million years ago were just as phantom and ungraspable as the events of now, or the events of the next ten minutes. It was perfect, the golden solitude, the golden emptiness, Something-Or-Other, something surely humble . . ." (Opening to verse #64)

Forges stoic steel bars, wrapping them in
warm, friendly wool

An allusion to an oral teaching of the Chinese martial art Tai Chi Chu'an, heard from my teachers Beth Rosenfeld and Lee Fife—"the body should be like a steel bar wrapped in wool" (that is, strong like steel from structural integrity and cultivated internal energy, but deeply relaxed and soft to the touch like wool)

we return to the destruction . . . sacralizing what was defamed

A reference to the Jewish holiday of Hanukkah and the events which inspired it: "What was the real miracle of Hanukkah? Some people say it was that a little band of Jewish rebels managed to defeat a numerically superior army of Greeks, an army who had taken over their land, and who had desecrated their Holy Temple. Others say it was the miracle of the oil; that the last little cruse of ritually prepared oil, somehow, lasted for the entire eight days it would take to make new oil for the Temple menorah. But maybe, just maybe, the real miracle was the miracle of re-dedication, of starting over and starting again. The Hebrew word *hanuk*, means 'to dedicate.' And when we use the word *hanukkah*, we are really talking about the 're-dedication' of the Temple after it had been desecrated, and to the 're-dedicating' of our lives to a relationship with the Source of All." (*The Hanukkah Miracle of Re-dedication*, Matisyahu and Netanel Miles-Yépez, *HuffPost* blog)

craft elephant legs for a steampunk Dali exhibit

A reference to the acclaimed painting of Salvador Dalí (1904-89) *The Temptation of Saint Anthony*, and its striking series of elephants with impossibly long, skinny legs.

Tears of a scarred phoenix, balm to the lesion

A reference to the healing properties of phoenix tears in J.K. Rowling's *Harry Potter* series.

RE-TURNING RE-MEMBERING

You are just as illusory as all partners attributed to Her Being

See note on *There's no* shirk- *no partnership- no other of course* (pg. 146-7)

He is your walking . . . your breathing

A play on a favorite *hadith qudsi* (non-Quranic statement of God recited through the prophet Muhammad) of the Sufis: ". . . When I love him, I am his hearing with which he hears, his seeing with which he sees . . ." (al-Bukhari)

This is not your body or mind, but the temple of the heart

A reference to the invocation commonly used by Inayati Sufis to open practice: "This is not my body, this is the temple of the heart." (See, *Sufi Prayers: The Prayers and Remembrances of the Inayati Sufis*, Netanel Miles-Yépez)

. . . toward God we turn

'Turning toward God' is a translation of the Arabic *tawbah*

161

and Hebrew *teshuvah*, both of which typically get translated as 'repentance.' This understanding of 'returning' is core to both Sufism and Hasidism. In the popular words of a Sufi poet: "Come, come back! Repent and come back again. Come, come whoever you are, infidel, fire worshiper, idol worshiper, come! Be not hopeless in our court. Even if you've broken your vows a hundred times, come, come again!" (*Come, Come Again!*, Abu Sa'id or Baba Afzal Kashani, commonly attributed to Rumi, in Omid Safi's *Radical Love*, 102-103) (For a Hasidic perspective, see the note on *'assemblies of raucous blazing hearts,* pg. 147)

VACANT FIREWORKS

. . . witness staff turn to snake and a bush on fire

A reference to two different points in the Biblical story of Moses: 1) when he saw the burning bush (Ex. 3), 2) and when the staff of his brother Aaron transformed into a snake, and devoured the snakes conjured by Pharaoh's magicians (Ex. 7:8-13).

'Let me take off these shoes and turn away from this place'

A play on the following passage from the Biblical account of the burning bush: "Do not come any closer," God said. "Take off your sandals, for the place where you are standing is holy ground." Then [God] said, 'I am the God of your father, the God of Abraham, the God of Isaac, and the God of Jacob.' At this, Moses hid his face, because he was afraid to look at God." (Ex. 3:5-6)

Tallis of light shrouding his face . . .

A reference to the following esoteric teaching from the masterpiece of Jewish mysticism the *Zohar*: "The Blessed Holy One took the light away from Moses, until he stood on Mt. Sinai to receive the Torah. Then the Blessed Holy One gave him back that light, and he wielded it his whole life long. The children of Israel could not come near him until he put a veil over his face—

as it is said: 'His face was radiant, they were afraid to come near him.' (Ex. 34:30) He wrapped himself in it as in a *tallis* (a prayer shawl); as it is written, 'He wraps Himself in light as in a garment' (Psalms 104:2)" (*Zohar: the Book of Enlightenment* (Classics of Western Spirituality), tr. Daniel Matt, 51-52)

... merkavah *turning*

". . . the term *merkavah* [Heb., lit. 'vehicle'] refers to an inner vehicle of consciousness that is used to journey through the many hidden dimensions of reality. It is also a code term for the *sefirot*, the divine qualities that make up the Tree of Life, which is the central map of consciousness in the Jewish mystical tradition" (*The Path of Primordial Light*, Zvi Ish-Shalom, 61)

A pillar of night, sparkling with specks of starlight

This is inspired by my teacher Zvi's frequent use of this same imagery. For example, while guiding his readers through an experiential exercise, he says: "Allow yourself to descend into the dense waters of Being. In these depths, the mind becomes quiet—there is no thinking, just more and more presence of pure nothingness, of emptiness, of blankness . . . it may feel as if you are surrounded by the deep, dark space of the vast night sky . . . In this profound state of silence, stillness, and deep peace, you will begin to experience a scintillating point of light, a star shining at the very center of all things, at the center of your being. A timeless, dimensionless star of light is discovered to be eternally shining in the vastness of inner space." (*The Path of Primordial Light*, Zvi Ish-Shalom, 128)

The dervish spins 'round the nail . . .

An homage to the training involved in learning the style of ritual Sufi dance known as 'whirling,' practiced by the Turkish Mevlevi Order. "Classically, the trainer would start the novice off, steadying him by having him turn with the big toe and second toe of his stationary left foot surrounding a large nail driven into the wooden floor of the *tekke* (Sufi gathering house), while the dervish would turn in place counterclockwise, using his right foot for locomotion" (*The Garden of Mystic Love, Volume II: Turkish Sufism and the Halveti-Jerrahi Lineage*, Gregory Blann, 26)

. . . I turned away from the fire, toward the gate of returning

This line points to the aforementioned Hasidic teaching connecting the story of the burning bush to the central role of *teshuvah* (repentance/return); see the note on *assemblies of raucous blazing hearts* (pg. 147).

The idea of gates (*sha'ar*) that open to various qualities, such as love (*ahavah*), awe (*yirah*), and returning (*teshuvah*) is expressed throughout Jewish thought. For example, the Talmud states: "The gates of prayer are at times locked and at times open. However, the gates of *teshuvah* are always open." (Eikhah Rabbah 3:44)

Finding Ani *to be* Ayin *(I to be Nothing) . . .*

A reference to a play on words employed in Hasidism to speak to the process of being 'dissolved in unity' or 'annihilated,' what Sufis refer to as *fana. Ani* (I) and *Ayin* (Nothingness) are spelled with the same three Hebrew letters, the only difference being the order of the second and third (A-N-I vs. A-I-N).

GODS OF BELIEF

. . . the God of my belief

This line, and in many ways the entire poem, is inspired by the aforementioned Ibn Arabi and his teaching on the 'Gods of belief': "According to Ibn-Arabi, as God necessarily transcends all limited names and forms, the heart of the ordinary human being cannot see or know God as such, but only the 'God of their belief,' the 'God' of which they have formed a limited idea (according to their capacity), that idea conforming to what has been revealed to them *from God*, who has also determined what the content of that belief should be!" (*In the Teahouse of Experience: Nine Talks on the Path of Sufism*, Netanel Miles-Yépez, 131)

. . . the pearl-clad princess

A poetic name for the Divine Presence, based on the Kedumah teachings use of the Hebrew words *penima* (princess) and *penina* (pearl) in relation to that Presence. (See, *The Kedumah Experience: the Primordial Torah*, Zvi Ish-Shalom, Ch. 7)

LIKE FINDING 20 BUCKS IN YOUR POCKET

You're taught the whole truth, then an angel comes, wipes knowledge away, with a press of their finger at your philtrum

A reference to the following Talmudic myth: "A fetus is taught the entire Torah while in the womb . . . And once the fetus emerges into the airspace of the world, an angel comes and slaps it on its mouth, causing it to forget the entire Torah." (Niddah 30b) Though not stated in this passage, a folk tradition developed and spread widely that rather than slapping, the angel presses their finger on a newborn's lips, as if to say 'Shhh,' and thereby forms one's philtrum (the vertical groove between the nose and upper lip).

There's that ringing if you listen real close.

An allusion to a practice shared between various sects of Yogis and Sufis in India, that of listening to the 'unstruck sound' (Sk. *anahad naad*), an inner vibration that sounds like a deep buzzing or continuous rainfall. (See, *Sufi Meditation and Contemplation: Timeless Wisdom from Mughal India*, tr. Scott Kugle with Carl Ernst, 96-104)

* ever so gently *

An homage to the seminal Centering Prayer instructions of Father Thomas Keating (1923-2018): "When engaged with your thoughts, return *ever so gently* to the sacred word." Of note is that this phrase has become emphasized in the practice of Centering Prayer, as an expression of the ideal overall orientation of gentle receptivity and surrender.

. . . the divine manner

This is one way to translate the Arabic *akhlaq Allah*, but many other viable translations exist, such as 'the ways of God' or 'divine virtues.' Though *akhlaq Allah* is an Islamic/Sufi phrase, the idea of embodying such a manner is also present within Judaism/Hasidism, and aptly stated in the Talmud: "Be similar, as it were, to Him, the Almighty: Just as He is compassionate and merciful, so too should you be compassionate and merciful." (Shabbat 133b)

. . . running and returning

This phrase is a translation of the Hebrew *ratso v'shov*. As the Hasidic lineage Chabad—that of Rabbi Zalman Schachter-Shalomi—defines it on their website: "*Ratzo* is a state of longing to cleave to G-d, the passionate desire of the soul to transcend its material existence, to 'run forward' and cleave to its Source. *Shov* is the soul's sober determination to 'return' and fulfill its mission in the body, the resolve to live within the context of material reality, based on the awareness that this is God's ultimate intent."

PHILOSOPHY TURNED MUSHY

Pondering Tantra, Vedanta, Chabad, the world as real, as illusory, as both or neither

An allusion to the philosophical doctrines of two schools of Hinduism (Shaiva Tantra & Advaita Vedanta), and Chabad Hasidism. In a simplistic way, the line correlates these traditions with their respective views on the 'reality of the phenomenal world.' As I understand it: Shaiva Tantra embraces phenomena as inseparable from the source of manifestation, and an avenue towards union with the divine; Advaita Vedanta rejects phenomena as fundamentally unreal, a distorting mask over the true ground and nature of reality; and Chabad Hasidism strikes a paradoxical middle ground, positing that 'from God's perspective' the world is unreal, only God exists, but that from the 'perspective of creation,' the world is undeniably real and demands us to interact with it as such.

THE MASTERFUL ACTOR'S GARB . . .

What's the difference between a saint and a phony, but masterful, actor who never breaks character?

This question, and in large part the poem as a whole, draws its inspiration from the Hasidic masterpiece "the Tanya," and its discussion of the *beinoni* (in-betweener) and the *tzaddik* (righteous person). As the Tanya puts it, a *tzaddik* is a wholly righteous person with no inclination to sin whatsoever, while a *beinoni* is one who never sins despite inclinations to do so. By these definitions, the Tanya's author, and founder of Chabad Hasidism, Reb Shneur Zalman, despite deservedly warranting a designation of *tzaddik* by most standards, identifies as a *beinoni*. In turn, he encourages his students to also strive to be *beinoni*, effectively deconstructing the category of *tzaddik* as a goal to pursue. Thus, the above question is in my own imagination a tongue-in-cheek way of asking: "Given that in terms of action a *tzaddik* and *beinoni* are identical, is there a practical difference between them?" (See, *A Hidden Light: Stories and Teachings of Early Habad and Bratzlav Hasidism*, Zalman Schachter-Shalomi & Netanel Miles-Yépez, 74-85)

INSTRUCTIONS TO THE VEGETABLE

A play on the title of the Zen classic *Tenzo Kyokun* (Instructions to the Cook), authored by the aforementioned Dōgen Kigen (See pg. 148). Of note is that both Zen and Sufism understand the communal kitchen as a ripe place for training, and employ cooking analogies in speaking to the spiritual path.

THE RAZOR'S EDGE

God is everything, all that is, was, will be!

"The name YHVH, the four-lettered name of God [is] the central Hebrew name of God in the Torah. It is simply the past, present and future tenses of the word 'to be' expressed in a verbal construct; HYH means was, HVH means is, and YHYH means will be . . . YHVH is the totality of all that ever is, was, and will be." (*The Kedumah Experience: the Primordial Torah*, Zvi Ish-Shalom, 53)

Where is She? Where we let Her in

A reference to the following story of the Hasidic master Reb Menahem Mendel of Kotzk (1787-1859), as I imagine it after hearing my teacher Pir Netanel retell it often: Once, the Kotzker asked a group of students, "Where is God?" to which they immediately responded, "Well, everywhere of course! The whole world is full of His Glory!" And in emblematic fashion, the Kotzker snaps back, "No you fools! God is wherever you let Him in!"

Fire boiling water, roasting lead and cinnabar til dragons lay with tigers

In writings and teachings on Daoist internal and external alchemy, each of these three pairs—fire/water, lead/cinnabar, tiger/dragon—represent the two fundamental energies of yang & yin. The line as a whole uses these traditional images to indicate the process by which these energies interact, both cosmically and individually, as they become purified and achieve a harmonious balance.

She wreaks havoc 'til victorious

An allusion to the common Hindu devotional phrase: *Jai Ma!* (Victory to the Mother!)

ASCEND TO DESCEND

Even your beloved teacher should not be in your heart at the hour of prayer

Within the Chisti order of Sufism from which my own lineage descends, envisioning one's spiritual guide (*tasawwur-i murshid*), and esoterically, even allowing for one's guide to practice through you, is a practice held in high esteem. Moreover, in addition to being a practice in its own right, the Chishtis encourage envisioning one's spiritual guide during almost all Sufi practice. (See, the *Kashkul Kalimi* translated in *Sufi Meditation and Contemplation: Timeless Wisdom from Mughal India*, Scott Kugle with Carl Ernst) Being stated in that context, this line is meant to stand in tension with that teaching, but certainly not negate it. What I'm trying to say (to myself, really) is: use the spiritual technology of envisioning your guide/s, as it can be incredibly helpful, but don't make them an idol; be ready and willing to let go of any superimposed form 'at the hour of prayer,' when the Real appears and seizes our imagination and hearts.

A SECRET TREASURE

I was a secret treasure that longed to be known

For the source of this phrase, see pg. 149.

. . . taste and know that God is good

A Hasidic maxim taken from Psalm 34:8, with a slight change; the original verse says 'taste and see,' rather than 'taste and know.'

Come and see . . .

The circle of companions whose voices makeup the *Zohar* uses the Aramaic *ta hazei* (come see) as a recurrent catchphrase to introduce mystical insights. (See, the *Zohar*, Pritzker Edition)

THE OUTER GATES, THE INNER SANCTUM

. . . But once they've answered, asked for the passwords . . .

An allusion to an early trend of Jewish Mysticism, circa 100 B.C.E to 700 C.E., known as 'Merkava Mysticism.' Many of the texts from this period describe an internal, heavenly ascent through 'the seven heavens/spheres,' culminating in a vision of 'the Heavenly Throne.' But as these texts describe, to pass through each threshold, the practitioner must provide the various angels who strictly guard the spheres with the correct 'passwords,' which are by and large exceedingly long, nonsensical strings of Hebrew letters. (See, Gershom Scholem, *Major Trends in Jewish Mysticism*, 49-52)

LISTEN: LOVE SINGS WITH EVERYTHING

The two songs quoted are Adele's *Rolling in the Deep*, and Ja Rule and Ashanti's *Always on Time*.

CALLIGRAPHIC BREATH

Inhaling—Allah, *Exhaling*—Hu

An allusion to the Sufi practice of *fikr*, inner recitation of sacred names and phrases in coordination with the breath. *Allah* and *Hu* form a central pair of divine names in Islam/Sufism, based on the nominative form of *Allah*, *'Allahu.'* Allah is the direct Arabic equivalent of 'God,' the supreme name encompassing all attributive names, and generally represents the transcendent aspect of the divine. And standing on its own, 'Hu' or 'Huwa' (lit. He) represents the immanence of divinity, the 'isness of Presence.'

. . . like a needle threading a pearl

A reference to the following line from one of the Tai Chi Classics and the translator's associated note: "Move the *qi* (internal energy) as in a pearl with nine bends; there is not the slightest place the *qi* does not reach . . . [Note] The pearl with a crooked passage is used here as a metaphor for the body and the maze of vessels and energy pathways, and the challenge of moving the *qi* through it. Legend has it that pearls such as this were made with one passage carved into nine bends . . . [making] the pearl very difficult to thread. One story portrays Confucius learning a secret for threading it from a young girl. She instructs him to tie a silk thread around an ant, and then tempt the ant to go through the pearl's passage by placing some honey at the far end of it." (*The Tajiquan Classics*, Barbara Davis, 128)

LINEAGE

. . . the chain

A literal translation of the Arabic *silsila*, a technical term referring to the initiatic 'chain of transmission' through which Sufi orders trace themselves, always back to the Prophet Muhammad and God.

. . . illuminated masters

See the use of this term in the prayer *Toward the One*, in the note on *The illuminated masters gather . . .* (pg. 142).

Aaauuummm Huuuuuuuuu

For an explanation of these two divine names/syllables, see the notes on *with a Big Bang* (pg. 144) and *Exhaling*—Hu (pg. 171).

Ever so gently

See the note on the same phrase (pg. 166-7).

EASY AS 1,2,3

Births the unbegotten 1

An allusion to the Quranic statement about God: "He begot no one nor was He begotten" (112:3)

Yin and Yang, Shiva and Shakti dancing

Both pairs, Yin and Yang & Shiva and Shakti, symbolize the archetypal division of manifestation into two primary forces—light and dark, transcendent and immanent, masculine and feminine, etc. The first derives from its common use in a variety of Asian religious thought, and the second stems from the Hindu tradition of Shaivism, in which these forces are depicted as the dance of the male-female couple Shiva and Shakti.

Love, Harmony, and Beauty

Hazrat Inayat Khan, the founder of Universalist Sufism, gave special attention to these three qualities and often spoke of them in conjunction. For example, see the note on *The illuminated masters gather . . .* (pg. 142).

ESCAPING WITHOUT ESCAPING

. . . our lives become loci for channeling Her beauty, grace, and care

On the human being as a locus of manifestation for divine qualities, see the note on *The unfurling of swirling cosmic lights* (pg.149)

. . . epistemologically reborn

A phrase inspired by my teacher Zvi. See the second paragraph of the note on *The four worlds become singular* (pg. 151).

THE RIDER, THE WITCH,
AND THE WHIRLPOOL

. . . flip the poles of consciousness—I influence everything, everything influences me

An allusion to the practice of 'reversing space,' as taught by Sufi teacher Reshad Feild. The following passage from his autobiographical novel describes a bit of what his teacher, 'Hamid,' taught him about this practice: "He [Hamid] had explained to me that the average human being believes that he or she is cause to something, and therefore everything starts with the ego center projecting itself outwards onto the screen of life . . . Hamid had also told me about another way of viewing life, by allowing oneself to be viewed . . . He then taught me an exercise for what he called 'reversing space,' which involved sitting very still, with all attention focused in the center of the chest, and slowly surrendering and realizing that: instead of looking you are being observed; instead of hearing you are being heard; instead of touching you are being touched; instead of tasting you are food for God and are being tasted." (*The Last Barrier*, Reshad Feild, 86-87)

RECOMMENDED BOOKS

ENGLISH TRANSLATIONS OF SUFI POETRY

Islamic Mystical Poetry: Sufi Verse from the Early Mystics to Rumi,
ed. Mahmood Jamal

Radical Love: Teachings from the Islamic Mystical Tradition,
ed. Omid Safi

Love's Alchemy: Poems from the Sufi Tradition,
tr. David and Sabrineh Fideler

The Drop that Became the Sea: Lyrics Poems,
Yunus Emre, tr. K. Helminski and R. Algan

'Umar Ibn Al-Fāriḍ: Sufi Verse, Saintly Life,
tr. Emil Homerin

Fakhruddin 'Iraqi: Divine Flashes,
tr. W. Chittick and P. Wilson

INTRODUCTIONS TO SUFISM

The Teahouse of Experience: Nine Talks on the Path of Sufism,
Pir Netanel Miles-Yépez

Gathekas,
Hazrat Pir-o-Murshid Inayat-Khan, ed. N. Miles-Yépez

Garden of Truth,
Seyyed Hossein Nasr

The Knowing Heart,
Kabir Helminski

Awakening,
Pir Vilayat Inayat-Khan

Introductions to Hasidism/Jewish Mysticism

God is a Verb,
David Cooper

Gate to the Heart,
Rabbi Zalman Schachter- Shalomi

Teachings of the Jewish Mystics,
Perle Besserman

The Essential Kabbalah: The Heart of Jewish Mysticism,
Daniel Matt

Chasidic Masters,
Aryeh Kaplan

Souls on Fire: Portraits and Legends of Hasidic Masters,
Elie Wiesel

A Heart Afire: Stories and Teachings of the Early Hasidic Masters,
Rabbi Zalman Schachter-Shalomi & Netanel Miles-Yépez

Hasidic Sufism

The Merging of Two Oceans: Nine Talks on Sufism & Hasidism,
Netanel Miles-Yépez

Kedumah

The Kedumah Experience: The Primordial Torah,
and *The Path of Primordial Light,*
Zvi Ish-Shalom

The Inayati-Maimuni Order is committed to a path of spiritual development based upon both Sufi and Hasidic principles and practices. In this order, the Sufi lineage of Hazrat Inayat Khan (1882-1927), the first Sufi master to bring Sufism into the West, has been joined to the Hasidic lineage of Rabbi Zalman Schachter-Shalomi (1924-2014), founder of the Jewish Renewal movement. But because it is not the first time that these two mystical paths associated with Islam and Judaism have been brought together, we endeavor to connect to and renew the spirit of the original Egyptian Sufi-Hasidism practiced by Rabbi Avraham Maimuni of Fustat (1186-1237), our forerunner, who successfully combined these paths as far back as the 13th-century. For this reason, we are called the Inayati-Maimuni *tariqa*, honoring both Hazrat Inayat Khan's vision of Sufism as a universal approach to spirituality and Avraham Maimuni's radical innovation which made a peaceful marriage between Jewish Hasidism and Islamic Sufism in a time of conflict between the Abrahamic traditions. Founded in 2004 by Pir Zalman Sulayman Schachter-Shalomi, *z"l*, and his *khalifa*, Pir Netanel Mu'in ad-Din Miles-Yépez, the community is currently led by the latter, and based in Colorado.

www.ingramcontent.com/pod-product-compliance
Lightning Source LLC
Chambersburg PA
CBHW021628120626
46545CB00002B/445